# NAVIGATING THROUGH EMOTIONS

A Journey from being an Emotional Fool to being Emotionally Intelligent

Dr. Pratik P. SURANA(Ph.D)

INDIA • SINGAPORE • MALAYSIA

ISBN 979-8-89233-520-1

My timeless inspiration of the person who inspired me
and continues to do every moment of my life

**Navigating through emotions**
**Complete guide for making your emotions work for you and not against you**

I dedicate this book to my late father Shri Prakashchandra SURANA, My mother Pushpa P SURANA, My parents Bai and Babuji, My in-laws Mr. Prakash and Mrs. Chandanbala Khinvasara, My Sister Pragati, My wife Anshima, My kids, Krisha and Meghav, All the well wishers who stood by our family in the darkest hours and expressed their solidarity with us.. All my friends and extended families who understood each of my emotions. Least to say my colleagues at Quantum who understood each of my emotions and ensured we grew together.

# Contents

Chapter 1

# Introduction

There was a lizard. She saw a cob and she felt hunger pangs. She ran after him but he was too quick for her. In her rush her tail was caught in a hole. She just couldn't free it. She was in a jam. A cockroach witnessed this. It forgot that the lizard was on the lookout for a prey and would be hungry. Without thinking about it, he went to her rescue. And of course the inevitable happened. The lizard was fond of cockroaches. She had a grand meal.

The cockroach died and its soul left his body. He was very unhappy. He went to the fly who was supposed to be a master in spirituality. He told her the whole story, cried for himself and was into self-pity. He told the fly that things have changed. People no longer care for good deeds.

The fly smiled gently. She said, "Come with me". They went to the lizard and she asked her, "Do you know why you are still stuck?" She answered shamefully, "I know, I went madly after the cob. A cute little cockroach came to my rescue, but I ate him up too. It's entirely my fault."

The fly again asked," But why are you still stuck? Do you understand my question?" The lizard now became defensive. "Can't you see that my tail is caught up?" She flared up. The Fly answered, with equal anger said,

"Are you out of your mind? You know the reason. Why don't you cut off your tail?" Again the lizard answered sadly, "But I love my tail" The Fly questioned her, "Even more than your life? Do you know what will happen in case you stay stuck there? You will die of hunger or become a prey to someone else! Are you stupid? Don't you realize that you should first try to free yourself?" Come out of your comfort zone and learn to endure the pains of your growth zone. You will grow a new tail eventually. You will always remember this lesson and be more careful hereafter."

Thus saying the fly signaled to the soul and they flew away to a more secure place. The fly asked the soul what he had learned from this. The soul replied," Now I understand that our own actions and we ourselves are responsible for our problems. If we want to get out of such a problem we can do it ourselves. We need to introspect why we got caught up in it. We must become aware of our flaws and try to change ourselves. We must accept and adapt to our situation. Our conditions don't change, it is we who have to change and fit ourselves into it. This is growth."

The cockroach also added that," I did not think for a second before I went to her rescue. I did not allow her to think for herself. I was in my own mode of "goodness". I now realize that I was doing it to satisfy my egotist need, not for the true purpose of helping. But you my dear fly have taught us both to think for ourselves and be aware and conscious of our reality. You have so easily made us mindful of recognizing our emotional reactions and perceive what is right and wrong!" We in this book are going to learn all those things the fly tried to teach the cockroach's soul and in the same simple manner. So let us start with our emotional world.

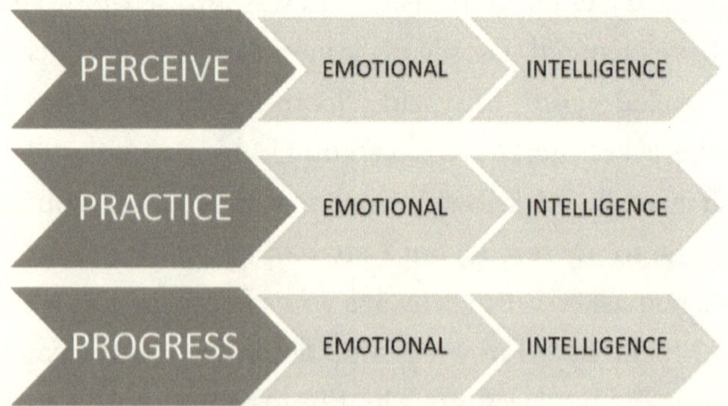

## OUR EMOTIONAL WORLD

Our emotional world is made up of broken hearts, edgy nerves, tightened throats! They take hold of us. According Vinciane Despret some of our emotions, precisely those we thought were a natural part of us, do not exist unless they have been inscribed into our subjectivity through culture. Thus they exist only within our relationships with others. Our emotions represent the way we perceive the world and try to make it or break it. Every person has his or her unique way of looking at things. Like, as we say beauty lies in the eyes of the beholder.

Our emotional world starts as soon as we take birth. We are the only ones that matter to us. Whenever we are in discomfort, we only have to cry and somebody is there to take care of our needs. We are the center of attention. The whole family runs around us and we become used to it. This also creates a sense of security which is vital for our emotional world. Availability of someone who loves and cares is a basic necessity to feel secure. Thus a baby is always pampered and looked after. Such a baby as he or she grows develops healthy ways and a healthy lifestyle. Much of this is dependent on "availability" of a caring person. This is the beginning of developing our emotional quotient.

There are many diverse facets to human nature. A person can be quite angry at times, and yet readily forget and forgive at other times. He is envious at times and affectionate at others. He acts selfishly at times, but he is also willing to make a sacrifice for others and step forward to assist them. Anger, joy, sorrow, jealousy, disappointment, fear, and a variety of other emotions are all examples of emotions.

We should be able to maintain a healthy balance between our emotions and thoughts. We are unhappy when someone hurts us. This is natural; nonetheless, we should be aware of how horrible it makes us feel. We become enraged when someone does something wrong, but we must not lose our cool. It's normal to want something, but we shouldn't be greedy in our pursuit of it. We can manage our emotions if we think properly. Coping with your emotions, being able to manage them, and expressing them in an acceptable manner are all part of emotional adjustment.

When we learn to manage our emotions, our personalities become more balanced, our capacity to comprehend people improves, and we are better able to cope with adversity. Then we are free of flaws like condemning others unnecessarily, calling them names, and refusing to accept their accomplishment. Our ability to relate to people improves as we get happier. We learn to be less obstinate.

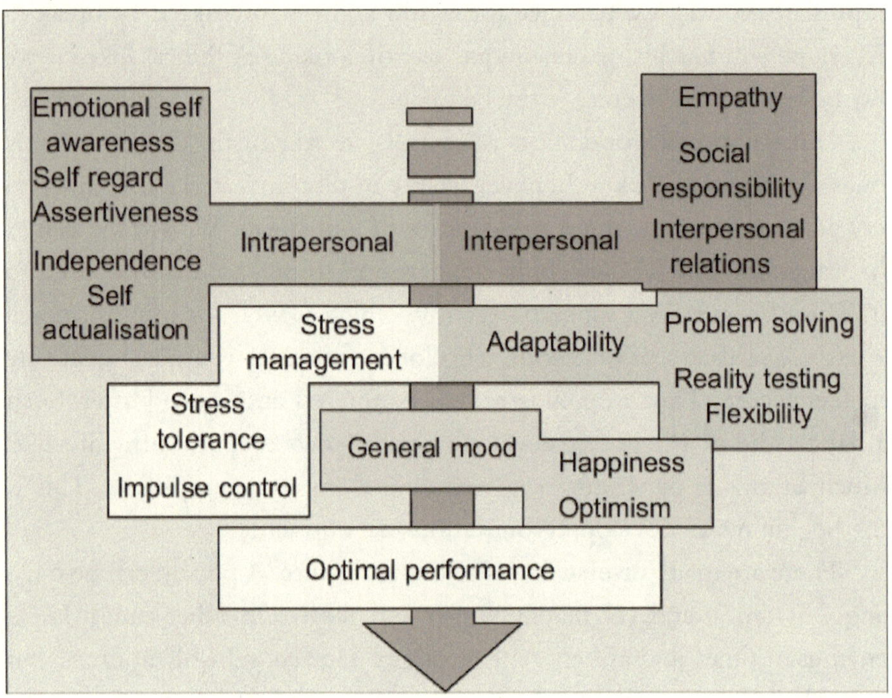


Give it a shot. What is the best way to study your emotions? Make a mental note of how you feel about the following and write it down.

(1) Your own actions from the time you get up until you retire to bed.
(2) Newspaper pictures of natural calamities.
(3) A cricket match reported in the newspaper.
(4) Resentment against your classmates/colleagues/friends.

There are many diverse facets to human nature. A person can be quite angry at times, and yet readily forget and forgive at other times. He is envious at times and affectionate at others. He acts selfishly at times, but he is also willing to make a sacrifice for others and step forward to assist them. Anger, joy, sorrow, jealousy, disappointment, fear, and a variety of other emotions are all examples of emotions

We should be able to maintain a healthy balance between our emotions and thoughts. We are unhappy when someone hurts us. This is natural; nonetheless, we should be aware of how horrible it makes us feel. We become enraged when someone does something wrong, but we must not lose our cool. It's normal to want something, but we shouldn't be greedy in our pursuit of it. We can manage our emotions if we think properly. Coping with your emotions, being able to manage them, and expressing them in an acceptable manner are all part of emotional adjustment.

When we learn to manage our emotions, our personalities become more balanced, our capacity to comprehend people improves, and we are better able to cope with adversity. Then we are free of flaws like condemning others unnecessarily, calling them names, and refusing to accept their accomplishment. Our ability to relate to people improves as we get happier. We learn to be less obstinate. What is the best way to understand our emotions?

Make a mental note of how you feel about the following and write it down.

(1) Your own actions from the time you get up until you retire to bed.

(2) Newspaper pictures of natural calamities.

(3) A cricket match was reported in the newspaper.

(4) Resentment against your classmates/colleagues/friends.

## A CHILD'S WORLD OF EMOTIONAL ADJUSTMENTS

Mostly Anna and Sarah progress at the same rate in their studies. The teacher compliments Anna's essay. Sarah becomes enraged and resolves not to talk to Anna. Here Sarah is under the influence of her ego which tells her wrong things. May be if she talks to the teacher or someone in authority the problem could get solved. But since she does not do this the problem remains.

Drake snatches Monty's pen and pencil from his backpack and places them in his pocket. Later, he apologizes to Monty and vows that he would not do it again. What made him do this? He understood the situation and the wrong thing he has done because he is emotionally stable. His reason makes him do the right thing.

Simmi wants to go to the market with her mother, but she had to go early for some reason. Simmi holds a grudge towards her mother. Later, she inquired of her mother as to why she had to depart so early. When she realizes why, her rage lessens. Why? Because she has the niceness to ask for the reason directly without any fear and gets her answer. Thus the problem between them is solved.

We must be aware of our own weaknesses. 'My handwriting is wonderful,' 'I am brilliant at arithmetic,' 'I appreciate science,' or 'I like poetry,' are common statements made by people. This implies that people's preferences, dislikes, and abilities may differ. We must gradually comprehend what we are able to achieve, just as we must gradually understand what we are unable to do. We may excel in one field, art form, or sport while failing miserably in another. We must be aware of both our flaws and our strengths in order to improve. Just because we can't accomplish something doesn't mean we shouldn't try to be the best at what we can.

We have the ability to change. There is no such thing as a totally good or evil individual. We must constantly consider our friends' good qualities or virtues first. We must assist one another in overcoming our weaknesses. It will be to our benefit if we discuss our defects as honestly as we discuss our strengths. Anger, like happiness and sadness, is a feeling. At some point in our lives, we all become enraged over something. When something does not go as planned or when we are offended, we become enraged. Similarly, we become furious when we witness someone being mistreated.

If we are angry frequently or cannot control our anger, it might have negative consequences for our health and mind. We become irritable and obstinate. Our willingness to cooperate and comprehend others deteriorates, and we cause harm to others. Headaches, lack of sleep, and dullness are some of the side effects.

## What Would You Do If You Were in This Situation?

(1) A dispute erupts between Robert and Abby over who gets to be seated on the first bench. Both of them are furious. They're on the verge of tossing each other's bags. How will they come to terms? They may make a deal that they take turns and solve the problem gracefully.

(2) Harry is eager to compete in a tournament, but he is shy. He is apprehensive about telling the teacher. He must learn to overcome his fear, give more importance to his career in sports and get the courage to speak up.

(3) Nancy's notebook was accidentally taken home by Rita. Rita immediately calls up Nancy, apologizes for her mistake and comes and returns the book, so things remain just as they were amongst themselves.

  (a) What factors influence the development of a balanced personality?

  Security, stability of thinking, rationality, flexibility and some control over emotions are necessary to develop a balanced personality.

  (b) Why is it that our attitude toward cooperation and understanding deteriorates?

We must take steps to rectify this. Irrational thinking which means thinking under the influence of emotions, because it takes us away from reality. This in turn pampers our ego and it becomes bloated. Thus our attitude becomes negative toward cooperation and understanding.

## What Should We Do Now That We've Discovered Our Character Flaws?

This entails learning to recognize our flaws, make a list of it and work on it with the help of a guide or counselor.

In her group, Nancy is the most vocal. Her friends started avoiding her because they never get the opportunity to interact with her. This is noticed by Nancy. She starts limiting how much she talked after that. "Stop me if I'm talking too much," she advised her companions. Nancy gradually learned to pay attention to others and changed her own behavior as a result. It's necessary to express one's emotions. We need to strike a balance between our thoughts and feelings. Anger must be managed; otherwise it will have negative consequences for our mind and body. We must be cognizant of both our weaknesses and our strengths. We can work to improve our nature's shortcomings..

It is possible to change aspects of our nature that disturb us and others. However, we must make a concerted effort to change them. Otherwise, these characteristics may manifest as personality faults. This we have discussed the natural course of learning to manage our emotions.

Imagine what kind of trauma an orphan or a neglected baby faces. This is also true in families where there are arguments in loud voices, resentment, anger or strong reactionary behavior. Faulty Family dynamics is a major threat to a person's emotional wellbeing. Such condition give rise to a syndrome well known as the King Baby Syndrome.

King Baby Syndrome is a condition of the brain, caused by childhood abuse, or trauma. The person concerned tries to take hold of all the control that they may not have felt in their childhood. They focus completely on themselves only. Their wants, their needs are above everyone else's and everything else.

It is just not possible for them to try and see things from others' perspective. Nor can they perceive others' opinion. In fact they are not even aware that there are other people like them who too can have an opinion themselves or a way at looking things.

They are extremely arrogant and look at each small or big event as a catastrophe and try to appear that they are very attentive and concerned (even if they're not.)

King Babies always want to cover up all their childhood pain because they feel overwhelmed with it and want to avoid dealing with it.

They will always try to show that they do not want to depend on others, admit their vulnerabilities, or face the pain they will have to face.

## AN UNHEALTHY COPING MECHANISM

In any kind of trauma or a mental illness, you have to cope up somehow.

This can be done in a healthy way, but people prefer to use unhealthy coping mechanisms like harming oneself, denial, and anger in order to deal with their pain.

King Baby Syndrome is another example of an unhealthy coping mechanism.

King babies deal with their past pain by totally neglecting it. They treat life like a never-ending party. Because when it comes to coping they need to process it. They are not at all interested in doing this. On top of it they expect others to run around them.

It is very painful for them to process things which need effort. If you try to force them they will simply start putting you out of their lives.

### Six Examples That Depict This Syndrome

Below, we list the six things that are commonly associated with King Baby Syndrome:

(1) **King Baby:** We have described this person above. He is egocentric, puts on a mask of confidence, but deep inside he is a small little child unable to come out. He is insecure and afraid."
King babies demand everything they want, when they want it, from everyone, and never give anything back" according to Tom Cunningham in his pamphlet.

(2) **The princess:** This is the female part of the King Baby. She is very similar because she sees everyone and every opportunity as objects meant to get her what she wants. On not

getting something she is quite capable of reacting strongly and she will throw a fit. When she walks in (an hour late), she expects everyone's attention and affection as well as admiration.

(3) **The ego tripper:** An ego tripper gets high on feeling good about himself and gaining praise from everyone around him, just like a marijuana or acid trip when the person gets high. If he slamming everyone around him. He is content as long as he believes he is superior to others. But if he does not receive the attention he seeks, he will become enraged.

(4) **The falsely humble:** This person does not appear to be a King Baby because he is always putting himself down, far below everyone else, but they do so to divert attention away from their underlying vulnerabilities, and they often thrive on the attention they receive.

(5) **The perfectionist:** This one appears to be doing okay at first look. Their house is in order, they appear to be a cohesive family, and they are always on time, but they thrive on the belief that they have a higher standard than the rest of the world. A perfectionist aspires to be placed on a pedestal. Furthermore, when they make a mistake (which they will), they are so embarrassed that they will criticise everyone else around them.

(6) **The clinging vine:** This person is so dependent on others that they expect others to do almost everything for them because it's too much or too difficult for them. Else they feel that they just can't do it. They'll flatter you more than they'll flatter themselves, but it'll be for the purpose of getting you to do whatever they want.

Some of their common characteristics-

1. They despise authority or believe that the rules do not apply to them.
2. They keep their emotions hidden.
3. They are constantly seeking approval.
4. They are terrified of being abandoned.
5. They are never satisfied/nothing is sufficient for them.
6. They are a materialistic bunch.
7. They will do whatever they can to escape failure and rejection, even if it means doing nothing.
8. They will have no faith in anyone.
9. They are egocentric to a fault (narcissistic).
10. They have a proclivity for jumping to conclusions.
11. If they are chastised or do not receive what they want, they have temper tantrums.

### King Babies in Relationships

King Baby Syndrome has an impact on everyone they come in touch with, not just the person who has the syndrome.

The family will find it difficult to get along with this individual and may be afraid to do much.

They frequently stifle teammate creativity and have been known to sabotage when they believe someone else is performing better than them.

Friends are often picked and rejected based on the amount of admiration and adoration they receive from the person.

Having any kind of relationship with a King Baby might be difficult, but it's vital to realize that they're not evil people; they just have a mental disorder.

King babies will never feel like they are enough, no matter how hard they attempt to make themselves feel better or cover up their anxieties with vanity and expensive items.

King kids are always comparing themselves to others and seeking to feel good about themselves. They feel defeated if they do not actually regard themselves better or if they do not at least feel good. King babies are the best example of a very poor emotional intelligence.

## HOW EMOTIONS CAN ASSIST US

What are your initial thoughts as you begin to read this? Are you interested in learning more? Are you hoping to learn anything new about yourself? Are you bored because you have to complete something for school and you're not interested in it — or delighted because it's a school project you like? Perhaps you're preoccupied with something else, such as excitement about your weekend plans or sadness over a recent split.

Emotions like these are a natural part of the human experience. They provide us with knowledge about what we're going through and assist us in determining how to respond.

From the time we are babies, we are aware of our emotions. Face expressions or actions such as laughing, snuggling, or weeping are used by infants and early children to express their feelings. They experience and display emotions, but they lack the ability to describe the emotion or explain why they are feeling that way.

We improve our ability to understand emotions as we become older. We can identify what we're feeling and put it into words rather than responding like children. We improve our ability to understand what we are feeling and why we are feeling it with time and practise. Emotional awareness is the term for this ability.

Emotional awareness aids us in determining what we require and desire (or do not desire!). It aids in the development of stronger bonds. That's because being aware of our emotions may help us communicate more clearly about our feelings, avoid or settle disputes more effectively, and move through uncomfortable emotions more quickly.

Some people are born with a stronger sense of feeling than others. The good news is that everyone can improve their emotional awareness. It only takes a little practice. However, the work is worthwhile. Emotional awareness is the first step toward developing emotional intelligence, a skill that can help people succeed in life.

Here are some fundamentals concerning emotions:

- Feelings come and go. Throughout the day, most of us experience a variety of emotions. Some are only a few seconds long. Others may loiter in order to develop a mood.
- Emotions can range from mild to severe, and everything in between.
- There are no good or bad feelings, but there are excellent and terrible ways of expressing (or acting on) emotions, and the intensity of an emotion can vary depending on the situation and the person. Learning acceptable ways to express emotions is a separate skill — managing emotions — that is built on a foundation of understanding emotions.

Everything is fine.

Some feelings are positive, such as happiness, love, confidence, inspiration, cheerfulness, curiosity, gratitude, or inclusion. Other feelings, such as anger, resentment, fear, humiliation, guilt, sadness, or worry, can appear to be more negative. Emotions, both pleasant and negative, are normal.

All emotions reveal information about ourselves and our circumstances. However, accepting what we feel might be difficult at times. We may condemn ourselves for feeling a specific way, such as if we are jealous. Instead than trying to convince ourselves that we shouldn't feel that way, it's best to pay attention to how we actually feel.

Avoiding bad emotions or acting as if we don't feel them can backfire. It's more difficult. We at Quantum Group, are committed to providing comprehensive training and resources to enhance your understanding of emotional intelligence, enabling you to perceive, practice, and progress in various aspects of your life.

## BUILDING EMOTIONAL INTELLIGENCE

Emotional awareness allows us to better understand and accept ourselves. So, how do you become more conscious of your feelings? Begin with these three easy steps:

1. Make it a habit to pay attention to how you're feeling in various scenarios throughout the day. You could discover that making plans to go somewhere with a friend makes you feel excited. Or that you're worried about an upcoming exam. Listening to music can help you relax, while an art show can inspire you, and a compliment from a friend can make you happy. Simply pay attention to whatever emotion you're experiencing and label it in your thoughts. It only takes a second, but it's excellent practice. Each feeling fades and makes place for the next.
2. Assess the intensity of the emotion. Take it a step further after you've recognized and named an emotion: On a scale of one to ten, rate how strongly you feel the emotion, with one being the mildest and ten being the most severe.
3. Tell those closest to you about your feelings. This is the ideal way to practise expressing feelings in words, a talent that can help us feel more connected to our friends, lovers or girlfriends, parents, coaches, or anybody else. Make it a habit to communicate your feelings with a friend or family member on a daily basis. You could discuss something highly personal or something that is just a common emotion.

When it comes to emotions, just like anything else in life, practice makes perfect! Remind yourself of this.

## THE ROLE OF EGO IN OUR EMOTIONAL WORLD

What exactly is the ego?

- The ego is a self-created identity made up of all of our beliefs about who we are and what we are.
- Our personality, talents, and likes/dislikes are all part of this.
- The ego is what keeps us locked away in our heads, disconnected from the present moment.
- The tale we tell ourselves creates and reinforces our identity. Our tales, on the other hand, are just that, Stories. They aren't the ones who make us who we are.

"The most common ego identifications have to do with possessions, work, social status and recognition, knowledge and education, physical appearance, special abilities, relationships, person and family history, belief systems, and often nationalistic, racial, religious, and other collective identifications," writes Eckhart Tolle. "You aren't one of them."

The ego is a part of the human situation, but it is not who we are.

We are usually focused with right and wrong, blame and guilt when we function from the ego. We are responding from a judgmental, rather than a loving, perspective. We're not behaving out of a sense of "how can I help" or "how can I provide"…

The ego enjoys being correct. This is how it keeps going. The issue is that it also prevents you from taking the steps necessary to get closer to love and truth. In this way, the ego is similar to a weed. It may have lovely blossoms for your inside garden, but if left unchecked; it can suffocate all of your other plants, leaving you in a tangle.

When you forgive, your heart opens up, and you let go of the desire to be "correct" and instead choose love. This is what it means to be in touch with your actual self. Forgive others as well as yourself.

Allow yourself to let go of the need to be right, to win, to be seen, and to be heard. Instead, pay attention.

The ego needs to be loved and validated, so it jumps up and down to prove itself. Our greater self does not require approval. It is love, as our higher self understands.

You create room to be seen and heard without expectation by becoming aware of the ego and its need to be seen, heard, and acknowledged. You can observe things as they are by observing without expectations. Because they don't meet your ego's standards, you view individuals as they are rather than through a projected sensation of lack.

In this place, you can also take a step back and examine who is or is not performing properly.

## SELF ESTEEM AND EMOTIONAL INTELLIGENCE

Emotional intelligence has been a popular topic in psychology, and various studies have been conducted on the subject.

In 1990, Mayer and Salovey coined the phrase "emotional intelligence," which they define as "the mental ability of humans to reason with emotions to enhance thought while encouraging intellectual and emotional growth." Individual differences in emotional intelligence have been discovered by many researches. The study of emotional talents as predictors of psychological well-being, health, and social functioning is the focus of these studies.

Emotional intelligence (EI) is described as the capacity to recognize, scrutinize, and transmit emotions correctly. Individuals who can understand and control their emotions have a more positive outlook on life and have better psychological well-being than those who can't.

Emotional intelligence is defined as a subject that aims to explain, comprehend, and interpret a person's feelings, joys, and ability status. Emotional intelligence is also defined as the ability to understand emotions in order to evaluate thoughts, behaviors, and arrange them in a way that promotes emotional and intelligent growth and maturity.

The concept of emotional intelligence lends fresh power to an individual's intelligence, which is based on conscious competition (personal performance), whereas recognition intelligence is a strategic capacity (long term capability). Because it concerns how individuals apply information in a direct manner, emotional intelligence allows it to foresee achievement. Emotional intelligence is a type of social intelligence that is used to predict achievement in specific areas such as school and work. In other words, it has the potential to guarantee ones and others' sentiments and joys.

Positive emotional intelligence is seen to be a strong predictor of greater psychological adjustment and self-esteem, whereas low emotional intelligence has been linked to depression.

Self-esteem is defined as an emotional response to a general feeling about oneself that is either favorable or negative. Self-esteem is characterized by Biabangard as a generic personality quality as well as a personal evaluation of worthiness.

Self-esteem is defined as a value that includes information within a person's self–imagination and is generated by the person's beliefs about all of his features, aspects, and characteristics.

As we enter the new millennium, the term "feeling" has taken on a new meaning. The term "emotional" refers to someone who is "markedly agitated in their feelings or senses." When a person feels the right emotion in the right situation and expresses it in the right amount, he is considered to be emotionally intelligent.

Adolescence is a critical period in which young people strive for identity and meaning in life, with emotions and self-esteem playing a key role. According to Goleman (1998), there is a worldwide trend for the current generation to be more emotionally afflicted than previous generations; lonelier and unhappy; more furious and rebellious; more impulsive. According to Swami Veerabhadra et al (2014), 63.38 percent of teenagers are emotionally immature. According to Shobha Nandwan and Kushagra Joshi (2010), 55 percent of teenagers have low emotional intelligence. Resmy José and Sujatha R (2012) discovered that 46 percent of teenagers are emotionally unstable, whereas Sharma Bharti (2012) discovered that 52 percent of adolescents are emotionally immature.

Emotional intelligence is defined as the ability to identify, analyze, control, and harness emotions in oneself and others in an adaptable manner, as well as to use emotion to aid cognitive function.

Self-esteem is defined as recognizing one's own worth, importance, and having the character to be responsible for ourselves and others. It doesn't mean that you think of yourself as the most important person on the planet; rather, it refers to how you feel about yourself and how much you value yourself.

Improved emotional intelligence has been linked to happier moods and higher self-esteem, according to research, since emotionally intelligent people are better at managing their emotions.

It is a skill that entails three processes: perception (or the ability to consciously recognize) and memory. When a person can accept his or her flaws while also recognizing his or her talents and positive characteristics, he or she will have a strong sense of self-worth and esteem. Emotional intelligence and self-esteem are linked, according to Schutte et al., (2002)

The main goals of this study are to see if emotional intelligence is distinct and useful in understanding the relationship between self-esteem and other demographic variables. It's also important to look into the extent to which people with high emotional intelligence have higher self-esteem, as well as the relationship between emotional intelligence and self-esteem and other demographic variables.

A descriptive cross-sectional survey was conducted to determine the association between emotional intelligence and self-esteem, as well as other demographic factors. The research was carried out in six schools in the Punjabi area of Faridkot. The study included 200 adolescents (14-16 years old) who were selected at random from several schools in the Punjabi district of Faridkot. Adolescents are defined as those who are between the ages of one and thirty-one years old on January 1, 1997, and December 31, 1999.

The subjects' data was collected using three different methods.

1. Data sheet for socio-demographics:

   Researchers created it to collect socio demographic data from people. It included 7 questions on age (birthdate), gender, standard/class, family type, family income (in rupees per month), mother's educational status, and father's educational status. This tool took approximately 2-3 minutes to administer in total. Subject experts determined that the tool's content was valid. The test–retest approach was used to determine reliability, which resulted in a score of 1.0.

2. The Emotional Intelligence Scale is a tool that measures your emotional intelligence

   The emotional intelligence scale (Schutte et al., 1998)[15] is a 33-item questionnaire designed to measure a person's capacity to recognize, understand, manage, and harness emotions in themselves and others. From strongly disagree to strongly agree on a five-point scale. Reverse scoring applies to items 5, 28, and 33. A score of 165 is the maximum possible. High emotional intelligence is indicated by a high score. Internal consistency ranges from 0.87 to 0.90 on this scale, with two-week test retest reliability of 0.78. (Schutte et.al, 1998). This tool took around 10 minutes to administer in total. Reliability was r=0.83 in the current investigation.

The Rosenberg self-esteem scale is a three-point scale that measures how confident you are in yourself.

The Rosenberg self-esteem scale (Rosenberg, 1965)[16] is a standardized, ten-item scale that is used to assess an individual's overall sense of self-acceptance and self-worth.Self-esteem is reflected in a high score. The current research reveals that emotional intelligence and self-esteem have a substantial beneficial link. This result is in line with what has been found in other studies. Lourdes Rey et al. discovered a link between emotional intelligence and teenage self-esteem and life satisfaction. Country and Chester (2005) did a study on emotional intelligence and self-esteem, and found that the two have a positive association.

Sameer (2008) conducted research in India on the association between self-esteem and emotional intelligence among trainees in the tsunami-affected coastal region of Kerala's Alappey district. Emotional intelligence and self-esteem were found to be positively associated, according to his findings.

Iram Abbass also discovered a favorable and significant link between emotional intelligence and self-esteem among Pakistani teenagers. Higher emotional intelligence has been linked to greater psychological functioning, according to Petrides and Furnham (2006)

Emotional intelligence has been linked to better empathetic perspective taking and self-monitoring in social circumstances, as well as more affectionate relationships, according to Schutte et al. emotionally intelligent persons have a better marriage relationship. Austin et al. discovered a robust link between emotional intelligence and happiness, as well as a congruent relationship between well-being and emotional intelligence.

The strong link between emotional intelligence and self-esteem could be due to the fact that emotionally intelligent people are more likely to have a surplus level of psychological well-being and a lower level of emotional shortage than people with poor emotional intelligence. Due to their capacity to effectively control (by identifying, analyzing, producing, regulating, and promoting) their emotions, emotionally intelligent people are able to maintain positive mental states. When a person accepts his or her flaws while still acknowledging his or her talents and positive characteristics, he or she will have a strong sense of self-worth and esteem.

Adolescents should be examined for emotional intelligence and emotional maturity on a regular basis, according to the study, in order to identify their emotional issues. Teachers, parents, and health-care professionals can be trained in a variety of strategies to help students maintain emotional stability and self-esteem. Psych education, therapy, meditation workshops, and other treatments may be given to emotionally immature adolescents to help them develop a positive self-concept and self-esteem, according to the study.

Thus the study concluded that Emotional intelligence and self-esteem are favorably and strongly associated. Emotional intelligence should be measured on a regular basis in adolescent kids because it impacts self-esteem and other characteristics. Educational interventions should be included in the curriculum to address emotional immaturity in school adolescents, and school health nurses can employ them in the classroom.

This study does not show any relation between gender, age, and other demographics as far as impact of EI and self-esteem are concerned.

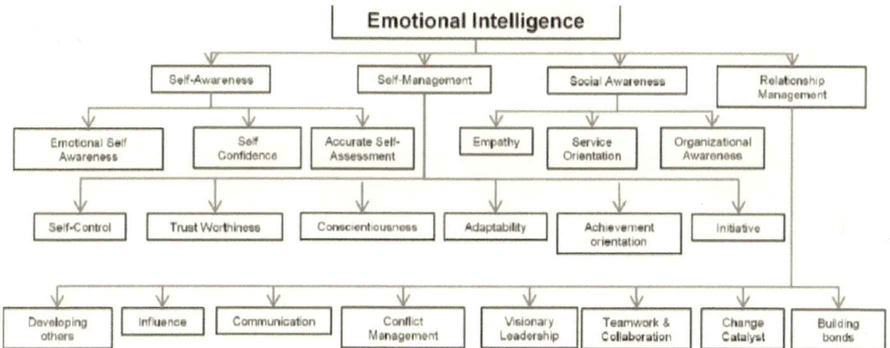


* * *

Chapter 2

# The Young Adult

This stage represents the bachelor student stage of life. This stage focuses on education and includes the practice of celibacy. The student goes to college or school acquiring knowledge of science, philosophy, scriptures and logic, practicing self-discipline, working to earn, learning to live a life of righteousness, morals, duties.

Erik Erikson was an ego psychologist who created one of the most well-known and significant development theories.

The stages that make up his theory are as follows:

- **Stage 1**: Trust vs. Mistrust
- **Stage 2**: Autonomy vs. Shame and Doubt
- **Stage 3**: Initiative vs. Guilt
- **Stage 4**: Industry vs. Inferiority
- **Stage 5**: Identity vs. Confusion
- **Stage 6**: Intimacy vs. Isolation
- **Stage 7**: Generativity vs. Stagnation
- **Stage 8**: Integrity vs. Despairng

During each Stage, There Will Be Conflict.

Erikson's theory builds on the previous stages and prepares the way for subsequent periods of development. Erikson felt that people go through a struggle at each stage that acts as a turning point in their development. These conflicts, according to Erikson, revolve around the development or lack it. Personal growth opportunities abound, but so does the risk of failure. People who successfully deal with conflict emerge from the stage with psychological strengths that will serve them well throughout their lives. They may not develop the fundamental abilities for a strong sense of self if they are unable to successfully deal with these disputes. A sense of competence, according to Erikson, inspires behaviors and acts. Erikson's theory is divided into stages, each of which is concerned with gaining competence in a certain area of life. The person will have a sense of mastery if the stage is managed properly, which is sometimes referred to as ego strength or ego quality. If the stage is not handled properly, the person will feel inadequate in that area of development.

| **Psychosocial Stages: A Summary Chart** | | | |
|---|---|---|---|
| **Age** | **Conflict** | **Important Events** | **Outcome** |
| **Infancy** (birth to 18 months) | Trust vs. Mistrust | Feeding | Hope |
| **Early Childhood** (2 to 3 years) | Autonomy vs. Shame and Doubt | Toilet Training | Will |
| **Preschool** (3 to 5 years) | Initiative vs. Guilt | Exploration | Purpose |

| Psychosocial Stages: A Summary Chart | | | |
|---|---|---|---|
| **Age** | **Conflict** | **Important Events** | **Outcome** |
| **School Age** (6 to 11 years) | Industry vs. Inferiority | School | Confidence |
| **Adolescence** (12 to 18 years) | Identity vs. Role Confusion | Social Relationships | Fidelity |
| **Young Adulthood** (19 to 40 years) | Intimacy vs. Isolation | Relationships | Love |
| **Middle Adulthood** (40 to 65 years) | Generativity vs. Stagnation | Work and Parenthood | Care |
| **Maturity** (65 to death) | Ego Integrity vs. Despair | Reflection on Life | Wisdom |

## A brief summary of the eight stages

| Psychosocial Stages: A Summary Chart | | | |
|---|---|---|---|
| **Age** | **Conflict** | **Important Events** | **Outcome** |
| **Infancy** (birth to 18 months) | Trust vs. Mistrust | Feeding | Hope |
| **Early Childhood** (2 to 3 years) | Autonomy vs. Shame and Doubt | Toilet Training | Will |
| **Preschool** (3 to 5 years) | Initiative vs. Guilt | Exploration | Purpose |
| **School Age** (6 to 11 years) | Industry vs. Inferiority | School | Confidence |
| **Adolescence** (12 to 18 years) | Identity vs. Role Confusion | Social Relationships | Fidelity |
| **Young Adulthood** (19 to 40 years) | Intimacy vs. Isolation | Relationships | Love |
| **Middle Adulthood** (40 to 65 years) | Generativity vs. Stagnation | Work and Parenthood | Care |
| **Maturity** (65 to death) | Ego Integrity vs. Despair | Reflection on Life | Wisdom |


## A brief summary of the eight stages

| Psychosocial Stages: A Summary Chart | | | |
|---|---|---|---|
| **Age** | **Conflict** | **Important Events** | **Outcome** |
| **Infancy** (birth to 18 months) | Trust vs. Mistrust | Feeding | Hope |
| **Early Childhood** (2 to 3 years) | Autonomy vs. Shame and Doubt | Toilet Training | Will |
| **Preschool** (3 to 5 years) | Initiative vs. Guilt | Exploration | Purpose |
| **School Age** (6 to 11 years) | Industry vs. Inferiority | School | Confidence |
| **Adolescence** (12 to 18 years) | Identity vs. Role Confusion | Social Relationships | Fidelity |
| **Young Adulthood** (19 to 40 years) | Intimacy vs. Isolation | Relationships | Love |
| **Middle Adulthood** (40 to 65 years) | Generativity vs. Stagnation | Work and Parenthood | Care |
| **Maturity** (65 to death) | Ego Integrity vs. Despair | Reflection on Life | Wisdom |

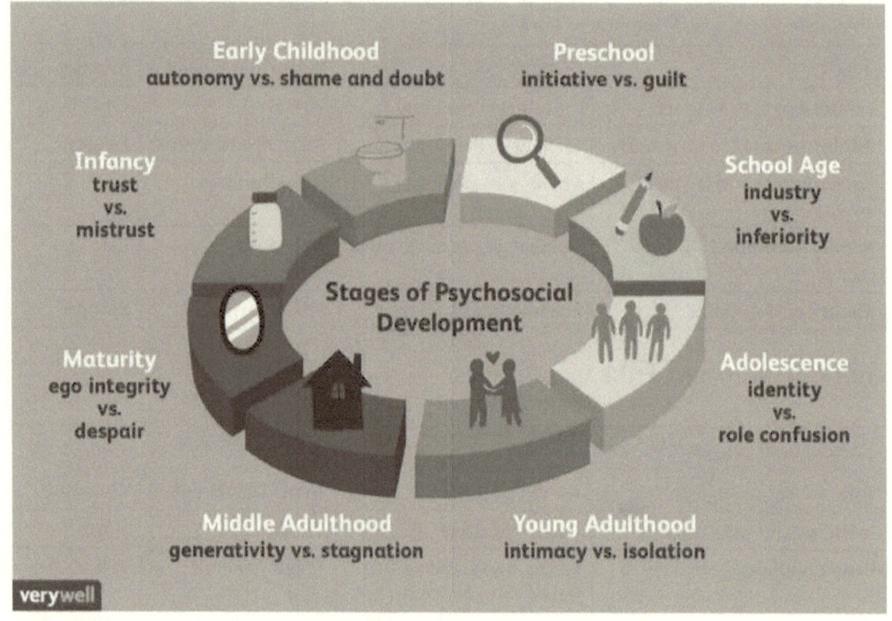


## A BRIEF SUMMARY OF THE EIGHT STAGES

### Stage 1: Trust vs. Mistrust

The most essential stage in life, according to Erikson's theory of psychosocial development, occurs between birth and one year of age. Because a newborn is completely reliant, the child's caregivers' dependability and quality are crucial in fostering trust.

The kid is completely reliant on adult caregivers for all they require at this stage of development, including food, love, warmth, safety, and caring. If a caregiver fails to provide appropriate care and love, the child will begin to believe that he or she cannot trust or rely on the people in their lives.

If a youngster builds trust successfully, he or she will feel safe and secure in the world. Children's sentiments of mistrust are exacerbated by caregivers who are inconsistent, emotionally unavailable, or dismissive. Fear and the perception that the world is inconsistent and unpredictable will result if trust is not developed. When caregivers provide consistency, care, and affection, children develop a sense of trust during the first stage of psychological development. Mistrust will result if this isn't done.

No youngster will ever develop a sense of complete trust or complete scepticism. Erikson believed that the key to effective development was achieving a balance between the opposing forces. When this occurs, children develop hope, which Erikson defined as "an openness to experience tempered by some fear of risk."

## Stage 2: Autonomy vs. Shame and Doubt

Early childhood is the subject of Erikson's second stage of psychosocial development, which focuses on children gaining a larger sense of personal control. Importance of Independence

Children are just beginning to obtain some independence at this stage of development. They are beginning to take basic acts on their own and making simple selections about their preferences. Parents and caregivers can help children develop a sense of autonomy by allowing them to make decisions and gain control.

### *Potty Instructions*

The main focus of this stage is for children to gain a sense of personal control over their physical abilities as well as independence. Potty training aids in the development of this sense of independence in youngsters.

Erikson, like Freud, believed that toilet training was an important part of the process. Erikson's logic, on the other hand, differed significantly from that of Sigmund Freud. Learning to control one's body functions, Erikson felt, contributes to a sense of control and independence. Gaining more control over food preferences, toy preferences, and clothes choosing are also significant occurrences.

### *Outcomes*

Children who struggle and are shamed for their mistakes may lose their sense of self-control. Success leads to sentiments of autonomy throughout this period of psychosocial development; failure leads to feelings of shame and mistrust.

### *Striking a Balance*

Children who finish this stage feel safe and confident, while those who do not are left feeling insecure and self-conscious. Erikson felt that striking a balance between autonomy and shame and doubt would lead to will, or the conviction that children can act with purpose, within reason and boundaries.

## Stage 3: Initiation vs. Guilt

During the preschool years, children go through the third stage of psychosocial development. Children learn to express their authority and control over the world by controlling play and other social interactions at this stage in their psychosocial development.

Children that succeed at this stage believe they are capable of leading others. Those who do not develop these skills experience remorse, self-doubt, and a lack of effort.

### *Outcomes*

The third stage of psychosocial development emphasizes the need for children to begin establishing control and authority over their surroundings. A sense of purpose emerges as a result of this stage's success. Children who try to wield too much power are met with criticism, which leads to feelings of guilt.

The ego attribute known as purpose occurs when a perfect mix of individual initiative and a willingness to collaborate with others is reached.

## Stage 4: Inferiority vs. Industry

The fourth psychosocial stage occurs in the early school years, between the ages of 5 and 11. Children develop a sense of pride in their accomplishments and talents as a result of social interactions. New social and academic demands must be met by children. Failure leads to emotions of inferiority, whilst success leads to feelings of competence.

### *Outcomes*

Parents and instructors who praise and encourage their children develop a sense of competence and confidence in their abilities. Those who receive little or no support from their parents, instructors, or classmates will have doubts about their ability to succeed.

Finding a balance at this period of psychosocial development leads to competence, a strength in which children acquire confidence in their skills to handle the responsibilities they are given.

## Stage 5: Confusion vs. Identity

The fifth psychosocial stage occurs throughout the frequently tumultuous adolescent years. This stage is critical in the development of a sense of personal identity, which will influence a person's behaviour and development for the rest of their lives. Teenagers must develop a feeling of self and individuality. Failure leads to role confusion and a weakened sense of self, but success leads to the ability to stay loyal to oneself.

Children explore their independence and build a sense of self during adolescence. Those who are encouraged and reinforced appropriately via personal discovery will emerge from this stage with a strong sense of self and sentiments of independence and control. Those who are unsure of their own views and desires will feel insecure and uncertain about themselves and their future.

### *What Exactly Is Identity?*

When psychologists discuss identity, they are referring to all of a person's ideas, ideals, and values that help shape and influence their conduct. After successfully completing this stage, Erikson defined fidelity as the ability to live up to society's standards and expectations.

While Erikson believed that each stage of psychosocial development was significant, he emphasised the development of ego identity in particular. During the identity versus confusion stage of psychosocial development, ego identity is the conscious feeling of self that we build via social contact and becomes a key emphasis.

## Stage 6: Isolation vs. Intimacy

Young adults require the development of close, caring relationships with others. Failure leads to loneliness and isolation, whilst success leads to close relationships. This stage encompasses the early adult years when people are experimenting with intimate connections.

Erikson felt that developing close, dedicated relationships with others was essential. Those that succeed at this level will develop long-lasting and stable partnerships.

### *Continuation of Previous Stages*

Keep in mind that each level builds on the skills you learned in the previous ones. Erikson thought that forming intimate connections required a strong sense of personal identity. According to studies, those who have a low sense of self have fewer committed relationships and are more prone to experience emotional isolation, loneliness, and despair.

When this step is completed successfully, the virtue of love emerges. It is characterised by the ability to build long-term, meaningful connections with others.

## Stage 7: Stagnation vs. Generativity

Adults must develop or nurture something that will outlast them, which they frequently do by having children or by making a beneficial change that benefits others. Failure leads to a shallow sense of connection in the world, whereas success leads to feelings of usefulness and accomplishment.

We continue to create our lives as adults, focusing on our careers and families. Those that succeed in this phase will feel as though they are making a difference in the world by being involved in their home and community. 2 Those who do not master this talent will feel unproductive and disconnected from the rest of the world.

When this stage is successfully handled, the virtue of care is realised. This stage emphasises being proud of your accomplishments, witnessing your children grow into adults, and building a sense of togetherness with your life partner.

## Stage 8: Integrity vs. Despair

The final psychosocial stage comes in old age and is centred on life retrospect.

People at this stage of development reflect on the events of their lives to see if they are satisfied with their lives or if they have regrets about the things they did or did not do.

Erikson's theory was unique among others in that it addressed development across the lifespan, including old age. Older people need to reflect on their lives and feel fulfilled. At this stage, success brings sentiments of wisdom, whereas failure brings feelings of regret, bitterness, and despair.

At this point, people look back on their lives and assess their accomplishments. Those who reflect on a life well lived will feel fulfilled and prepared to face the end of their lives with confidence. Those who look back with only regret will be afraid that their life will end without completing the tasks they believe they should have completed.

We at Quantum Group provide insights into Erikson's stages of psychosocial development, acknowledging that each stage is associated with unique emotional challenges. By understanding these stages, participants gain insights into how age-related conflicts might manifest and impact emotional intelligence.

## ONE DAY AT A TIME

I had been working in a place for twelve years.. I was assigned a new task and it also meant promotion plus a hike in salary. I was very happy and I started working on the project enthusiastically. I felt proud of myself and also I basked in the sense of importance it was giving me. Things were okay for a while. Then I started facing problems. I could not get the right kind of material and the thing could not be done on time. Besides, the quality was compromised. I had worked really hard but things just went against me. Finally I accepted my failure to the authorities. They decided to fire me and instead asked me to resign. I was given 2 days to decide. I was completely frustrated, all the while thinking of the various things that went against me and the failure. I lost confidence and was worried to death about what to do next. My reputation was already spoiled in the company and friends too avoided me. I started thinking about suicide and read articles which stated the most easy and painless ways of dying. I was flabbergasted, worn out at the edge of my tether when I suddenly remembered a message I had read on whatsapp. It was the story of an incidence which happened in a school. A very naughty boy stuck a label on the back of another student which read "I'm stupid". Al the class was laughing at this and whispering about it. The little boy was not aware of this label and was concentrating on the studies. Next was the class for maths. The teacher gave an example and asked the boys to come ahead and solve it on the board. Nobody could do it and all were silent. This little stood up amongst the laughter of others still ignorant of the label.

He solved the problem on the board and the teacher removed the label. He addressed the whole class and said," This is what I would like to tell the class. Firstly throughout your life people will keep on labeling you. If the boy knew about the paper on hid back he would not have come to solve the problem. All you have to do in life is to ignore the labels people give you and use every chance to go ahead in life and progress.

The second thing is it is clear that he has no real friends who would tell him about the paper. It does not matter how many friends you have, but it certainly matters who is a loyal friend. If you don't have friends who support you even behind your back, who watch you, who defend you and take genuine care of you are better off. So please do not put tags on others which can destroy them and will not get you anything."

This story suddenly seemed to wake me up and I started seeing things clearly. My thoughts changed. I felt hopeful, and my fear reduced. It made me relax. I had wanted to die. But now there was hope.

Then one day I read an article that lifted me out of my despondence and gave me the courage to go on living. I shall never cease to be grateful for one inspiring sentence in that article. It said: 'Every day is a new life to a wise man.' I typed that sentence out and pasted it on the windshield of my car, where I saw it every minute I was driving. I found it wasn't so hard to live only one day at a time. I learned to forget the yesterdays and to not-think of the tomorrows. Each morning I said to myself: 'Today is a new life.' I'm happy and fairly successful now, and I'm full of energy and zest for life. I know now that I will never be terrified again, no matter what life throws at me. I'm relieved to know that I won't have to be concerned about the future. I've learned that I can only live one day at a time, and that "a wise man's every day is a new life."

Who do you suppose wrote this verse:

> Happy the man, and happy he alone,

He, who can call to-day his own:

> He who, secure within, can say: "To-morrow, do thy worst, for I have lived to-day."

Don't those words have a contemporary ring to them? Nonetheless, they were composed thirty years before Christ's birth by Horace, a Roman poet.

**Interpersonal Dynamics:** Understanding how age-related conflicts can influence interpersonal dynamics is crucial for developing strong social skills. Quantum Groups' programs address the impact of age on communication styles, empathy and relationship building, enhancing participants' ability to navigate social interactions at various life stages.

**Self-Awareness Across Lifespan:** The training emphasizes Self-Awareness across different life stages. Participants learn to recognize and understand the emotional challenges specific to their age group, fostering a deeper understanding of themselves and others.

One of the most terrible aspects of human nature, in my opinion, is that we all have a tendency to put off life. Instead of appreciating the roses that are growing outside our windows today, we are all daydreaming of some heavenly rose garden beyond the horizon.

## Why Are We Such Knuckleheads, Such Tragic Knuckleheads?

The story of an alcoholic who was able to break the shackles he himself had put in his hands when he got trained of these mechanisms at Quantum Group.

## THE BEST GIFT OF MY LIFE

'Mistakes are painful when they happen, but years later, a collection of mistakes is called experience, which leads to success!'

Today is my 54th birthday. These words kept ringing in my ears. They aptly suited the situation. I have celebrated so many birthdays but today was something very, very, special! I have an immeasurable gratitude to my God for making this day for me. No words can describe just how I feel. I am completely at a loss as to how I must thank my God and so many others who have helped me experience this intense satisfaction!

Today I got back the trust of my only child which I had lost 20 years ago. He had stopped talking to me because of the fact that I was a drunkard. His hateful eyes, his distrustful attitude the pain and the misery he suffered, the disregard were always haunting me. I have had a hard time facing this and also maintaining my sobriety. I have often cried with the agony and my friends who understood my predicament stood beside me. We had drifted apart for so long that I had no hope of regaining a place in his heart again......

The seed of this was sown long back. I was studying for my twelfth standard. The cheerful atmosphere, the pleasant banter, the laughing and the noise was all very familiar. College had started from today and we boys were eager to find new girls. Roaming around with friends we tried to spot new admissions especially of course girls and it was at this time that I spotted her. She was fair, with a very sweet face, long thick hair and a beautiful smile! Oh how my heart fluttered, and raced and then felt as if it will stop! I just couldn't take my eyes off. I suddenly became conscious that I was staring at her. I dropped my eyes and moved ahead.

The next day again I saw her in the library and tried to make small talk. She responded and was amused by my shyness. But she was very friendly. Soon we became friends and then also knew that we were very much involved in each other. We met every day in college and even after college. We used to meet surreptitiously on Sundays. Whatever pocket money I got was now at her disposal. She used to have more money than me. It was so nice and we were so happy. It became impossible to be without her. Whenever she went to her native place, it was torture for me to be away from her for so long.

After my twelfth I took admission for B.Pharm. She continued in the same college. Both of us studied together and were always together. The only times I could stay away was when I had parties with my friends. This was occasional, but I looked forward to this and in spite of the fact that she disliked my drinking, I continued.

Two years went by and things were as good as can be. But one day my world came crashing down. She went away to her native place, her native place because her home people had come to know about our affair. She somehow sent me a message that they were getting her married. I rushed to her native place and through a friend we met. I promised to get a license to get married in court and immediately did so. But alas they shut her up in the house all in filmy style and I returned empty handed. Oh what a 'Majnu' I had become! I got an excuse to drink. I was Devdas and Majnu etc. all rolled into one. A friend took me out and we drank whiskey for the first time. That day I slept soundly and could forget my woes. It soon became a habit and eventually I was caught up into the clutches of Alcoholism.

She was soon married and moved to Lukhnow. I found out everything about her and her husband. I was 'wronged' by her and fate and God! Poor old 'Me!' I drank more and more to forget it all. At the same time I loved to hold on to that image of 'Devdas' the wronged one. I expected alcohol to wipe out something I had a stronghold on. This would never happen but it was a game I played with my own self. Later I came to know that this was my 'Alcoholism.' This 'Poor me' image, this self-pity, this drinking and many more. Somehow I completed my studies and got a Government job. I was indeed lucky; but did not have the gratitude to accept it. Thus I started earning and drinking. These were my careers. Be it at home or in office; sneaking drinks during lunch hours or remaining absent from work. Being a Government job memos and warnings were all I got, but did not lose my job. Not happy with anything I wanted to hurt her. I sent a letter to her husband telling him everything of our affair. I addressed it to his bank where he worked. Soon her cousin informed me that she is having problems in her married life.

Another shock was awaiting me and I blamed myself for it. I got to know that she had committed suicide by hanging herself because her husband had started troubling her and was suspicious. The world went blank! I was so shocked and numb, I couldn't think. I can never forget the misery and the pain. I knew that I was responsible. Now my drinking increased with a vengeance. I could not look at myself in the mirror. I felt ashamed, hurt, angry, and unhappy and tortured myself with these thoughts. I could not even decide whether I wanted to live or die.

My cousin talked to me and pleaded with me to stop drinking. My parents, my brothers were all worried, but never attempted to say anything aloud due to fear. I would get very belligerent and aggressive if anyone so much as mentioned alcohol in front of me. I finally agreed and stopped. They were all happy but even minus the alcohol, I was as bad, as pigheaded, as aggressive and egoistic. I still had that 'Poor me' image, very close to my heart. Eventually I got married and remained away from drinks for a span of four years. A chance allusion to my previous girlfriend's death was enough for me to collapse. How fickle things were with me! This happened so often in the later years. Only just a small something or nothing was enough to start off my drinking career. My wife and my only son were continuously dreading that moment and did everything in their power to avoid such situations. Because drinking daily was bad in itself but when there a was reason it was worse. Once my son over heard somebody saying that a certain girl has stopped talking to her father because he is a drunkard. My son who was at an impressionable age followed her example. From that day on he stopped talking to me. But I had nothing but a few abusive words hurled at him in fits of anger.

My family started getting worried and decided to get me admitted in a rehab. They had fixed everything and my elder brother came to my workplace to get a long leave granted, but I shooed them away as if they were dogs. I refused to get admitted. My wife was desperate and she somebody told her about AA. She went to their office and that evening two people visited me. I listened to them only because I wanted to put off getting admitted and here was a good reason for me.

That day I went for my first AA meeting instead of taking a drink. I listened to them all; felt I could 'handle' myself better. Came out and went to the usual shop where I purchased liquor. But something happened. I suddenly felt I could not drink. The shopkeeper asked me if there was a problem. I lied to him, saying I had no money. He offered to loan me a bottle but I refused and left the place abruptly. Now I understand how God helps when you really mean to do something that is right. I went home and my wife opened the door. She was so happy to see me sober that she hugged me. But I got angry because as usual I misunderstood her affection. I thought she did it just to see if I was drunk! Later she showed mw a bottle of sleeping tablets and told me that my son and my wife had planned to end their lives on that day if I would have come drunk! This hit its mark and I thanked God for saving them and me. I can never get over for His Grace for me and my family.

I attended a meeting the next day again and my life just changed. My desire for drinking seemed to evaporate into thin air. I have not had a drink from that 10$^{th}$ day of March 1999.

Recovery for me was not as easy as it seems. I had to struggle hard to be away from that first drink and also working on so many of my characteristics. I was told that this is "Alcoholism' which means Alcohol + ism. The 'disease' includes alcohol the chemical as well as the ism which means 'I' 'Self, and 'Me.' I learned to understand these concepts and continue to do so even today. It was for me to awaken this happiness. For I have learned this lesson in life—

If you want to awaken happiness in the world around you, start by living a life that makes you happy, and then radiate your happiness outward. If you want to eliminate suffering, start by eliminating the dark and the negative in yourself and then radiate the positivity in you. Truly the greatest power you have in this world is the power of your own self- transformation It starts with one in the mirror.

Today after so many years I have had the pleasure of becoming a friend to my son who is now grown up. He was still not talking to me, but today on my 54th birthday he came all the way from Mumbai to greet me. When he hugged me all the pain, the agony, the misery in my life dissolved. I have received the Best Gift of my life!

This is where once again we at Quantum enter again.As an individual will progress through Erikson's stages, they encounter significant life changes. Quantum Group focuses on developing participants' adaptability, helping them navigate transitions and cope with the .emotional aspects of change, thereby contributing to higher emotional intelligence.

We at Quantum Group adopt a life-long learning approach, recognizing that emotional intelligence is not a static trait. The training encourages continuous self-reflection and skill development across different stages of life, aligning with Erikson's concept of ongoing personal growth.

## THE CONCEPT OF ONE DAY AT A TIME

What Does It Mean to Take One Day at a Time?

If you've ever been to treatment for drug or alcohol addiction or know someone who has, you've probably heard the phrase "live one day at a time." The statement is more than just a common encouragement; it has deep meaning, reflecting an individual's thanks for their sobriety and its current value. Exploring this frequent addiction recovery slogan and the significance of putting it into practise will help us live each day as it comes in order to stay sober and apprecia**tive.**

**"Living One Day at a Time."**

The expression "live one day at a time" is attributed to Alcoholics Anonymous and its "Big Book," even though it is not from one of the 12 stages. It comes from the original AA philosophy, which states that each person has a 24-hour period of sobriety. This essentially means that each person has a daily responsibility to feed their spiritual needs, which includes maintaining their sobriety. There is no cure for addiction; there is just a responsibility to oneself to be sober each day. This permits people in recovery to focus on the present moment rather than a long-term commitment to sobriety. Sobriety for today is a much simpler pill to take than sobriety for the rest of one's life, and it allows a person to feel at ease with their recovery goals.

## Being Present During the Recovery Process

To "live one day at a time" means to concentrate on the present moment rather than the past or future. Recovering addicts are likely to feel guilty and ashamed about their previous addictive actions, which can lead to relapse. In addition, recovered people may be uncertain about their future and fearful of the unknown, which can be a trigger to use. Focusing on the current goals and mission allows these persons to work on establishing helpful coping skills today, so they are prepared for the future and capable of dealing with the past.

## Taking One Day at a Time as a Goal

Not only is a person promising to live sober today, but they are also committed to do everything it takes to stay sober for the following 24 hours. These obligations include the following:

- Maintaining a positive outlook
- Tackling one issue at a time
- Increasing one's knowledge in some way
- React to others in a friendly manner and do good for them.
- Through contemplative techniques, a focus on loving oneself is emphasized.
- A readiness to attempt new things outside of one's comfort zone
- One problem at a time; one day at a time

Individuals are bombarded with feelings they have been avoiding through active addiction during addiction treatment and recovery. Dealing with all of the emotions that arise can be difficult, overwhelming, and virtually impossible. Taking rehabilitation one day at a time also entails coping with these feelings as they arise. It's far easier to deal with current problems than it is to become stressed by worrying about all of the problems. When a person focuses on the task at hand rather than worrying about tomorrow's problems, they are more likely to complete the task at hand and be prepared for the next day as it arrives.

## USING MINDFULNESS TO REMAIN IN THE PRESENT

To stay present, it takes more than repeating the slogan "live one day at a time." It takes a willingness to stay focused as well as a dedication to a new way of thinking and seeing things. It's a lot simpler to say than it is to do. Mindfulness meditation is one practise that can assist a person in recovery learn to stay in the present moment. This is meditation in which the inner focus is on current emotions, issues, and goals. Meditation, with practise and patience, can help to alter a person's thinking and help them stay in the present moment, resulting in a successful long-term rehabilitation.

To strike a balance between all this is a difficult task. It is an unusual skill that you need to learn.

By enrolling in Quantum Groups' programs, you'll not only gain a deeper understanding of emotional intelligence but also acquire the tools and skills necessary to perceive, practice, and progress in various facets of your life. This investment in your emotional wellbeing can lead to increased self-confidence, improved relationships, and overall success in both personal professional endeavors.

We at Quantum Group recognize the profound impact that age-related developmental stages, as outlined by Erik Erikson, can have on Emotional Intelligence (EQ). Here's how their programs can assist in understanding and navigating age-related conflicts within the context of Eriksonian psychosocial development.

A beautiful lotus will emerge out of the sloth of unskilled, eager to learn and a motive of bringing about a change in themselves

We at Quantum group try to give different approaches to achieve this goal.

- **Life-Long Learning Approach:** We at Quantum Group adopt a life-long learning approach, recognizing that emotional intelligence is not a static trait. The training encourages continuous self-reflection and skill development across different stages of life, aligning with Erikson's concept of ongoing personal growth.
- **Multi-Generational Understanding:** The programs foster an understanding of emotional intelligence across generations. By appreciating the unique perspectives and emotional needs of different age groups, participants develop a more inclusive and empathetic approach to interpersonal relationships, both personally and professionally.
- **Practical Application in Various Settings:** We at Quantum Group integrates Eriksonian principle into practical scenarios, helping participants apply their understanding of age-related conflicts and emotional intelligence in real-life situations, whether it be in workplace, family or social setting.

* * *

Chapter3

# Nuances of Emotions and Emotional Intelligence

At Quantum, we believe in cultivating self-awareness through engaging exercises. These exercises are in the form of some tests, games cultivating awareness and understanding the basics of self-awareness. Attention, concentration, practicing mindfulness, dealing with the ego and it's fundamentals to develop a strong and emotionally resilient person as given in the following chapter.

## ATTENTION AND EI

The science of attention has advanced well beyond vigilance in recent years. According to science, these abilities determine how well we accomplish any work. We do poorly if they are stunted; if they are muscular, we can flourish. Our ability to move quickly in life is dependent on this delicate ability. While the connection between attention and greatness is sometimes concealed, it pervades practically everything we strive for. This adaptable instrument is embedded in a plethora of mental functions. Comprehension, remembering, learning, feeling how we feel and why, reading emotions in others, and communicating seamlessly are just a few of the fundamentals.

This intangible aspect in effectiveness allows us to perceive the rewards of improving more clearly this mental faculty, and learn how to use it more effectively. Typically, we register the finished products through an optical illusion of the mind of attention—our excellent and poor ideas, a knowing wink or an appealing grin, the whiff of a cup of coffee in the morning—without perceiving the ray of consciousness itself.

Though it has a significant impact on how we negotiate life, attentiveness in all of its forms is important. Our trip begins with an examination of the fundamentals of attention. One of these is heightened alertness. Cognitive science investigates a wide range of topics.

Comprising concentration, selective attention, and open awareness, as well as the manner in which the mind directs its attention internally to monitor mental activity.

Such fundamental mental mechanics serve as the foundation for vital abilities. There is a sense of self-awareness, which promotes self-management. There's also empathy.

These are the foundations for interpersonal skill. These are the principles of emotional intelligence.

As we'll see, a lack of strength in this area can damage a person's life or profession.

## CONCENTRATION AND EI

Strengths contribute to fulfillment and success. As we move beyond these fields, systems science takes us to broader bands of emphasis, look around us, tuning us in to the complex mechanisms that define and restrict our world. Such an external emphasis encounters a hidden challenge is tuned in to these critical systems: Because our brain was not designed for such tasks we're stumbling. However, understanding the workings of a system is aided by system awareness.

All of this boils down to three things: inner, other, and outside concentration. A well-lived life necessitates that we be agile in each. The good news about focus originates in neuroscience labs and school classrooms, where the findings point to ways we might improve this critical mental muscle.

Like a muscle, if it is not used properly, it will wither; if it is used properly, it will grow.

We'll show how sensible practice can help us strengthen and refine our attention muscle, even if we have focus-deprived brains.

Leaders must have all three types of focus in order to achieve results. Inner attention allows us to be more aware of our intuitions, guiding ideals, and making better decisions. Other emphasis strengthens our bonds with the individuals in our lives. And having an outward focus allows us to navigate the greater world. A leader who is tuned out of his internal world will be rudderless; one who is blind to the world of others will be clueless; and those who are oblivious to the bigger systems within which they operate will be caught off guard.

Not only leaders gain from a balance in this triple concentration. We all live in perilous situations, filled with the tensions, competing aspirations, and enticements of modern life. Each of the three types of attention can assist us in striking a balance that allows us to be both joyful and productive.

Attention, derived from the Latin attendere, which means "to reach toward," connects us to the world, influencing and defining our experience. "Attention" supplies the mechanisms "that underpin our awareness of the world and the deliberate management of our thoughts and feelings," write cognitive neuroscientists Michael Posner and Mary Rothbart.

Then there are the fundamentals of attention, the cognitive muscle that allows us to follow a tale, complete a task, learn, or create. As we'll see, the infinite hours young people spend staring at technological gadgets may help them gain specific cognitive skills in various ways. However, there are concerns and issues regarding how those same hours could result in impairments in basic mental functions.

Rapport necessitates shared attention—mutual focus. Given the sea of distractions we all face on a daily basis, the necessity to make an effort to have such human moments has never been higher.

## THE DEPLETION OF ATTENTION

There are the expenses of adult attention decrease. A few years ago, you could prepare a five-minute film for your presentation at an ad agency, says an advertising rep for a prominent radio network in Mexico. You have to keep it to a minute and a half today. Everyone starts looking for messages if you don't get them by then. Our focus is always battling distractions, both internal and external. The question is, how much do our detractors cost us? When I recognize that my mind has been somewhere else during a meeting, a financial firm executive told me, he wondered what chances he would be been missing right now.

Patients inform that they are "self-medicating" with medicines for attention deficit disorder or narcolepsy to stay awake at work. If he didn't take this, he wouldn't be able to comprehend contracts, a lawyer says. Patients used to need a diagnosis for such prescriptions; presently, many of those drugs are common performance enhancers. A growing number of kids are faking attention deficit issues in order to obtain prescriptions for stimulants, a pharmaceutical route to attentiveness.

All of this was predicted by Nobel Laureate economist Herbert Simon in 1977. He warned in his book about the emerging information-rich world that what information eats is "the attention of its recipients." As a result, a plethora of information leads to a scarcity of attention."

Distractions are classified into two types: sensory and emotional. The sensory distractors are simple: as you read these words, you tune out the blank margins that surround this text. Consider the sensation of your tongue against your upper palate for a moment—just one of an unending stream of incoming inputs your brain filters out from the constant wash of background sounds, forms and colors, tastes, scents, sensations, and so on. The second type of temptation is more frightening: emotionally charged signals. While it may be easy to focus on answering your email in the midst of the hustle and bustle of your local coffee shop, if you overhear someone mention your name (potent emotional bait, that), it's nearly impossible to tune out the voice that carries it—your attention reflexively alerts to hear what's being said about you. Forget about that email.

## MINDFULNESS AND EI

Mindfulness is the discipline of becoming more fully aware of the present moment—without judgement and completely—rather of ruminating in the past or projecting into the future. It often entails heightened sensory awareness (noticing your breathing, sensing your body sensations, etc.) and being "in the moment."

If you are experiencing thoughts that bring you extreme discomfort or unease, it may be time to start a mindfulness practice to help you return to the present moment, which can greatly reduce your stress level.

While mindfulness has its roots in Eastern philosophy and Buddhism, it is not need to be religious. Anyone, regardless of religious beliefs, can benefit from mindfulness. There are some indications that mindfulness practice may be beneficial in your life. You might wish to give mindfulness a try if you have any of the following symptoms: You are experiencing sensations of anxiety or depression. You are easily distracted or find it difficult to concentrate. You're stressed. You have a difficult time being compassionate to yourself. You have a problem with overeating or excessive snacking. You have a tendency to dwell on negative emotions. Your interpersonal interactions are not as tight or as strong as you would like. The essence of our experience is change. Change is incessant. Moment by moment life flows by, and it is never the same. Perpetual fluctuation is the essence of the perceptual universe. A thought springs up in your head and half a second later, it is gone. In comes another one, and then that is gone too. A sound strikes your ears, and then silence. Open your eyes and the world pours in, blink and it is gone. People come into your life and go. Friends leave, relatives die.

Your fortunes go up, and they go down. Sometimes you win, and just as often, you lose. It is incessant: change, change, change; no two moments ever the same. We cover up those basic goals with layers of surface objectives. We want food, wealth, sex, entertainment, and respect. We even say to ourselves that the idea of "happiness" is too abstract: Look, we are practical. Just give us enough money and we will buy all the happiness we need. Unfortunately, this is an attitude that does not work.

Examine each of these goals and you will find that they are superficial. You want food. Why? because I am hungry. So you are hungry—so what? Well, if I eat, I won't be hungry, and then I'll feel good. Ah ha! "Feel good": now there is the real item. What we really seek is not the surface goals; those are just means to an end. What we are really after is the feeling of relief that comes when the drive is satisfied. Relief, relaxation, and an end to the tension. Peace, happiness—no more yearning. So what is this happiness? For most of us, the idea of perfect happiness would be to have everything we wanted and be in control of everything, playing Caesar, making the whole world dance a jig according to our every whim. Once again, it does not work that way. Take a look at the people in history who have actually held this type of power. They were not happy people. Certainly, they were not at peace with themselves. Why not? because they were driven to control the world totally and absolutely, and they could not. They wanted to control all people, yet there remained people who refused to be controlled. These powerful people could not control the stars. They still got sick. They still had to die. You can't ever get everything you want. It is impossible. Luckily, there is another option. You can learn to control your mind, to step outside of the endless cycle of desire and aversion. You can learn not to want what you want, to recognize desires but not be controlled by them. This does not mean that you lie down on the road and invite everybody to walk all over you. It means that you continue to live a very normal-looking life, but live from a whole new viewpoint. You dothe things that a person must do, but you are free from that obsessive, compulsive drivenness of your own desires. You want something, but you don't need to chase after it. You fear something, but you don't need to stand there quaking in your boots. This sort of mental cultivation is very difficult. It takes years. But trying to control everything is impossible; the difficult is preferable to the impossible. Wait a minute, though. Peace and happiness! Isn't that what civilization is all about? We build skyscrapers and freeways. We have paid vacations, TV sets; we provide free hospitals and sick leaves, Social Security and welfare benefits. All of that is aimed at providing some measure of peace and happiness. Yet the rate of mental illness climbs steadily, and the crime rates rise faster. The streets are crawling with aggressive and unstable individuals. Stick your arms outside the safety of your own door, and somebody is very likely to steal your watch! Something is not working. A happy person does not steal. One who is at peace with him- or herself does not feel driven to kill. We like to think that our society is employing every area of human knowledge in order to achieve peace and happiness, but this is not true. What we need to develop is resilience.

## OUR EGO AND EI

Purpose will assist you in accomplishing life-changing work. According to Holiday, the first step is to ask yourself "why do I do what I do?" If you do not know the answer to this question, you should spend some time determining it. The majority of individuals do not live intentionally. They travel aimlessly through life, seeking the next type of fulfillment and wondering why they aren't happy or getting what they want. They drive to a work they despise in order to pay for the car that transports them there, as well as the house they abandon during the day to commute to that employment. While the ego craves the security of a "secure" employment, purpose, as well as the best things, occurs outside of one's comfort zone.

On the other hand, many harmonious and effective individuals have discovered that answering the following questions enables them to live purposefully: Why do I do what I do? What kind of person am I? To what end am I working? Once one has chosen critical work over ego, how does one select what critical work to pursue? Bill Walsh, the coach who elevated the 49ers from the NFL's poorest club to the Super Bowl, is an excellent example of someone who prioritizes vital tasks. He was not preoccupied with some nebulous concept of "winning." He was well aware that concentrating on the fundamentals and honing them would result in success. He could influence what the team did and how well they worked, but he couldn't predict when the next win would occur. He was more concerned with effort (the part that was within his control) than with outcomes (which were out of his control). His criteria were modest and pragmatic rather than fantastic, but by applying them, as the proverb goes, "the score takes care of itself." John Wooden, the Hall of Fame college basketball coach who led his team to ten basketball championships in twelve years, had a similar perspective. These coaches demonstrated clarity, discipline, and perseverance on their path to mastery. They were clear about their mission, and their work brought them delight.

The Greeks coined the term Euthymia, which refers to our awareness of our own path and our ability to stay on it without becoming diverted. Prioritize your objectives clearly and then adhere to them. True confidence is earned through dedication; it is earned through discipline and mastery. One crucial lesson to remember is that enthusiasm does not aid critical task. It necessitates deliberation, not blind emotion, or else it succumbs to ego delusions. Without a connection to reality, a project cannot prosper. People that are passionate will tell you everything they intend to achieve, but they will never be able to demonstrate progress, because there is rarely any. They talk a lot but accomplish little. People that are purpose-driven do not need to talk about their work since the results will speak for themselves. It's acceptable to be enthusiastic, but do it with restraint. Execute with distinction. Maintain your humility; recognize that you will always have more to learn:

> The vital work that you wish to undertake will necessitate your consideration and deliberation. Pass on the enthusiasm to the amateurs. Make it about what you feel compelled to do and say, not about what you value or aspire to be.

Understand your ego, but after you've chosen to manage it and pursue your mission, be prepared for others who will attempt to sabotage you. We have for reference Jackie Robinson, who showed tremendous discipline in the face of hardship. As the first African American to play Major League Baseball, he faced open racism from fans, coaches, and other players while on the field while batting. Robinson would not have had the impact he has today if he had reacted to these injustices with his ego; he was motivated by a greater cause.

The one thing we can be certain of when commencing on an attempt is that there will be difficulties and that we will almost certainly be treated poorly. Two things to remember in these situations:

(1) When others treat you unjustly and unfairly, it degrades them, not you;

(2) Choose living time over dead time.

The second point requires additional discussion. Malcolm X spent years in prison. He read voraciously while there and emerged a far more informed guy than when he arrived. He had little control over his circumstances, but he could choose what to do while he was in there. Many people enter prison, but some take the opportunity to learn from their mistakes and improve their life upon release, while others re-enter shortly thereafter.

Alive time is time spent actively utilizing and developing your time; dead time is time spent passively. While we may not always have the ability to control our circumstances, we can always choose whether to spend our time living or dead. From Nazi concentration camps, Viktor Frankl was able to refine his theories of meaning and suffering. While a prisoner of war, Francis Scott Key wrote what would become the United States' national song. The book leaves an unanswered question:

> "...this is not the end of your life. However, it is a point in your life. How are you going to use it?"

Remain a student at all times.

In our Quantum Foundation's Mission One Million initiative, we actively explore the importance of emotional literacy. It's all about embracing a mindful approach to personal development and fostering emotional intelligence within our community."

The greatest leaders and thinkers throughout history have all been life students. They have an uncommon interest about life and the discipline to remain perpetually learners. Many people get overconfident in one field and lose sight of how little they know about everything else. The ego attempts to identify you with success by preventing you from learning more, yet learning is necessary, particularly in the beginning.

When you are first starting out, you must remember that you are not as good as you believe you are, your attitude is probably out of date or incorrect, and the information you received in books or school is out of date or incorrect.

Numerous elements will influence your performance as a newcomer, one of which is your willingness to listen to feedback, particularly critical input. Let's describes how an amateur gets defensive in the face of unfavorable input, whereas a professional relishes the opportunity to learn more. It exemplifies the concept of a true professional through the example of Kirk Hammett, lead guitarist of the heavy metal band Metallica. After being hired by Metallica, he immediately sought out a teacher to help him improve. Metallica went on to become one of the world's most successful bands, yet throughout this success; Kirk maintained a humble demeanor and continued to learn.

"If you are not continuing your education, you are already dead."

Hammett exemplified the characteristics of a true student:

A genuine pupil is similar to a sponge. Absorbing, sifting, and hanging on to what he can hold. A student is self-critical and self-motivated, constantly striving to increase his comprehension in order to progress to the next topic, the next challenge. A true learner is also his or her own instructor and critic. There is no place for ego in that.

To achieve excellence and to sustain it, you must adopt a student mindset. You must constantly be learning. Everything in life teaches you something, but ego gets in the way of the possibilities you've had or will have. Your ego will tell you that you are unqualified to complete an internship. The ego is averse to menial work because it believes it is too good for it. People who live with purpose see beyond this and focus on what is truly important, believing in what they must do. Take advantage of the opportunity. Consider an internship. Make the time and effort necessary to learn. Consider the long term; this investment will pay out in the long run:

Humility is what keeps us there, concerned that we lack sufficient knowledge and must continue to learn. The ego races to the finish line, rationalizes that patience is for losers (mistaking it for a weakness), and feels we are good enough to give our gifts a chance in the world.

Consider the larger perspective of life to cultivate humility. Consider the grandeur of the cosmos, the numerous galaxies that surround us, and how little you are. Recognize that you are also a part of this huge cosmos, and your mission will become more apparent. Looking into the night sky, as well as thinking about all the people and events that have come before you and all that will come after, can assist with this. Purpose appears to flow freely to those who take the time to consider the big picture.

The stoics coined the term sympatheia to describe this state of mind, which translates as "a sense of connection with the cosmos." This relationship prompts the question, "Who am I?" What am I doing and why am I doing it? We need to go in detail about how material prosperity might detract from this worldview. Allow your ego to persuade you that the world revolves around you. Purpose will be revealed to you through time if you actively seek it out, which is also a part of the stoic view: "Purpose deemphasizes the I." Purpose is about pursuing something greater than oneself, as opposed to self-indulgence."

Determine and pursue your objective, and then go about your task. Why you should create it rather than feign it: Can you picture a physician attempting to make do with less? Therefore, why would you attempt anything else?

Continue to be a continual learner even after—and perhaps especially after—your major triumphs. Eliminate what is superfluous. Maintain an open mind. Establish goals and live a purposeful life.

## SPEAK AND THINK LESS; ACT MORE

When you begin to live with purpose rather than passion, your ego begins to shrink, and you develop the peaceful confidence Seneca referred to as Euthymia: having a sense of your own path and avoiding distractions from externals. As you speak less and perform more, you will develop this serenity while working, which will assist you in maintaining your meaningful work:

You become aware that everything requires effort, and that effort might be rather difficult. However, do you truly comprehend? Do you have any idea how much work will be involved? Not work until you gets your big break, not work till you establish your name, but work, work, work, for the rest of your life.

While speaking is natural and universal, silence is becoming increasingly rare in today's environment. Your ego will tell you that you require external validation, but genuine confidence does not require verbal communication; it creates results. Talking suffocates action. Sit quietly and concentrate on your task. Don't allow yourself to be distracted by social media and the news and instead concentrate on your task. Observe how much better you become:

They quietly toil away in the corner. They channel their inner anguish into creation—and ultimately into stillness. They operate without regard for the impulse to seek attention. They are not very chatty. And they are unconcerned about the perception that others, out in public, are soaking up the limelight and thereby getting the better bargain (which they do not).

Too much talking and pondering saps the energy you may be putting into your work. While we do need to think at times, such as when picturing goals, spending too much time thinking and discussing what we are going to do reduces our likelihood of really doing it. Where are the outcomes? Maintain an emphasis on execution. Consider when necessary and then get to work. Individuals who live with a purpose recognize that they are not working to retire and spend their days on their couch. They are pursuing something greater than themselves, which provides them with confidence throughout their lives:

When confronted with a new task, do you attempt to discuss it or do you confront it full on?

Excessive thinking can also lead to living with what psychologists refer to as a "imaginary audience," Many teens experience this, and many adults continue to do so. It's the notion that others are observing and thinking about you even when they are not. It's the teenager who misses a week of class due to their embarrassment over spilling juice on their pants and believing that the entire school is discussing it. That is not the case. This is your fictitious audience. People do not care as much about you as you believe, which is a comfort. Because the majority of people are consumed by their own life, take some time to rationalize your views and then return to work. The ego adores and feeds on the imaginary audience, therefore keep the broader picture in mind, let go of your wandering thoughts, and bring yourself into the present moment:

It requires guts to live clearly and in the present moment. Do not dwell in the veil of abstraction; rather, live in the tangible and real, even if it is uncomfortable. Participate in the events occurring around you. Consider it, and make adjustments for it."

In a nutshell, we assert that we must control our egos or risk having them overpowers us. Consider Coach Bill Walsh, who concentrated on the fundamentals and led the NFL's poorest club to the Super Bowl. As Metallica's Kirk Hammett put it, be a perpetual student, soaking up everything around you like a sponge, aware that there is always more to learn. Along with living with purpose and remaining a learner, place an emphasis on completing the job rather than seeking recognition, allowing your confidence to shine through your accomplishments.

Stoicism practice can help you more effectively apply the principles included within each subject. Now, go out and do the life-changing work that you were born to do.

## EI AND RESILIENCE

Resilience is a muscle that must be exercised. Flex it sufficiently and it will require less effort to overcome emotional setbacks.

Emotional resilience is not about victory. It is the ability to power through a storm while maintaining a constant sail. As a result of living in an era of technological innovation, we must adjust to changes that have never occurred in our lives before every ten years. From rigorous digitization to social media's 24/7 influence, from changing professions to adapting to Gen Y's habits, it's only normal to feel emotionally tethered at times.

Emotional resilience is a way of life that is inextricably linked to self-confidence, self-compassion, and improved cognition. It is the means through which we empower ourselves to view adversity as 'temporary' and continue progressing in the face of pain and suffering. (2003) (Marano).

Emotional resilience, in a broad sense, refers to our ability to bounce back from a stressful encounter without allowing it to impair our internal motivation. It is not a "bend but do not break" characteristic; rather, resilience is accepting the fact that 'I am broken' and growing with the fractured bits intact.

When we are resilient, we not only adjust to stress and disappointment, but we also have the insight to prevent choices that would put us in such situations in the first place. Consider the following illustration: Mr A is a computer engineer, a trustworthy employee, a devoted husband, and an excellent boss. Mr A is punctual and engaged in his work. He is quick to learn from his errors, never procrastinates, and so never misses a deadline, as many of his friends do. He is content with what he has accomplished thus far.

Mr A possesses emotional fortitude.

## Emotional Resilience Elements

Emotional Resilience is composed of three components — these are the pillars upon which we can develop or improve our resilience. The three elements, often known as the three dimensions of emotional resilience are as follows:

1. The Elements of Nature: Physical strength, energy, excellent health, and vitality are all necessary components.
2. The Element of Mental or Psychological Well-Being: Adjustability, attention and focus, self-esteem and self-confidence, emotional awareness and regulation, self-expression, and thinking and reasoning abilities are all included.
3. The Social Constituents: Interpersonal relationships (at work, with a partner, with children, parents, friends, and in the community, for example), group conformity, likeability, communication, and cooperation are all included.

Resilience is the capacity to continue functioning competently in the face of significant life "stressors".

With the appropriate knowledge, training, and drive, emotional resilience can be built. Whether confronted with workplace risks, navigating a troubled relationship, or navigating the ups and downs of parenting a small rebel at home, emotional resilience enables you to not only deal with the problem efficiently, but also protects you from emotional catastrophe.

Online training programs offer courses specifically designed to assist students in developing emotional resilience. They assist a significant number of leaders and professionals by utilizing practical, evidence-based tactics that are aimed at assisting professionals in improving their personal resilience, leadership abilities, and team resilience.

Accepting that emotional resilience is inextricably linked to other spheres of life is a critical component of developing it. For instance, developing resilience at work will result in more resilience in personal relationships, and vice versa. Whether or not the training is focused at improving performance in a specific area, it is certain to have an effect on other areas of life as well.

A resilience training program aims to increase emotional resilience by focusing on the following:

### *1. Self-Awareness is the first step.*

The capacity to tune into our own emotions, psychological problems, and worldview. We develop a better knowledge of how our moods influence our actions as a result of increased self-awareness.

Rather than seeking assistance from others or blaming the world for our woes, self-awareness empowers us to seek solutions within. By increasing our awareness of our inner world, self-awareness enables us to grow in capability and cognition.

### *2. Perseverance*

Resilience training teaches an individual how to maintain the consistency and commitment necessary to keep trying. Perseverance, whether dealing with external stressors or internal issues, keeps the inner motivation alive.

### 3. *Emotional Regulation*

Individuals with greater emotional and self-control abilities can divert and alter their emotions. They are less likely to succumb to stress or allow it to negatively affect their life. They will pause before leaping and will not rush to conclusions.

### 4. *Adaptive Thinking*

Alice Boyes (2014) stated in one of her Psychology Today posts that flexible thinking is a critical part of mental health that adds to a person's personal and professional success.

It is a very effective social skill that combines optimism, adaptability, logic, and optimistic thinking. A person who possesses these talents or has developed them via training or experience will undoubtedly be more emotionally robust and balanced in life.

### 5. *Relationships with Others*

Maintaining healthy personal relationships is both a result of and a prerequisite for emotional resilience. If we possess the ability to form strong interpersonal ties, whether professional or personal, we have already taken a significant step toward living a robust life.

Jennie Phillips, Ph.D. in Social Sciences and Education from the University of Ontario, stated in one of her blogs (2014) that developing great interpersonal interactions broadens our perspective - it alters our perception of the world and of ourselves.

We are social creatures, and being surrounded by other people provides us with the power to conquer obstacles, suffer hardships, and progress as a result of them. To develop emotional resilience in a broader context, we must be able to enhance our existing interpersonal relationships and be receptive to developing new ones.

## Management of Stress and Emotional Resilience

Coping with stress, or more precisely, efficiently coping with stress, directly contributes to the development of resilience.

The entire concept of emotional resilience is based on our ability to deal with stress and get back on track.

Being entangled in the daily stresses of life can play a significant role in our loss of emotional resilience. We become more perceptive, hypersensitive, and emotionally imbalanced as a result. Even a minor change in plans might cause us anxiety and distress.

According to research, resilient individuals can cope with stress more efficiently. They are more likely to absorb lessons from traumatic experiences than to be overwhelmed by them, since they can bounce back from any stressful scenario with positive energy and confidence (American Psychological Association, 2012).

The American Psychological Association broadened its research on emotional resilience to include individuals of various ages and victims of various types of stress.

The Resilience Booster Social Media Campaign unearthed fascinating statistics about how poverty and unemployment have a detrimental effect on both children and their parents' emotional resilience. Through an in-depth research-based practical toolkit for parents, this programme teaches guardians how to assist their children in dealing with external stress and developing immunity to it (American Psychological Association, 2015). By far, one of the most successful public interest projects for fostering and enhancing emotional resilience has been this one.

## Cycle of Stress and Emotional Resilience

How to Build Emotional Resilience and Protect Your Mental Health (Book)

Dr. Harry Barry, a GP and expert in Cognitive Behavior Therapy (CBT), just published a book on emotional resilience titled 'Emotional Resilience: How To Protect Your Mental Health' (2018).

Originally published in May 2018, this book is without a doubt one of the most comprehensive and popular works on emotional resilience.

Dr. Barry describes emotional resilience as the 'building blocks of life' in his book, using understandable concepts and practical examples.

According to him, the reason some people are better at managing stress than others is because of their resilience. Exposure to toxic stress (also known as burnout) elicits strong emotions, and our coping systems are activated instantly to deal with the circumstance (Barry, 2018).

Dr. Barry asserts that resilient individuals are more adept at employing these coping techniques and so more comfortable adapting to adversity.

Additionally, he said that while some people are born with greater resilience and emotional balance than others, we are all capable of becoming into emotionally robust and psychologically mature human beings given the proper instruction.

The book is a gold standard in applied psychology and mental health therapies from which we may all benefit. The book also acts as a training handbook for anyone interested in developing their resilience power through practical and simple activities that are mostly based on CBT concepts.

The book's intervention tactics are founded on three themes (Barry, 2018):

- Cognition - the manner in which we think
- Perception - the manner in which we perceive and assess things
- Action - our response to it

The book's concepts aim to improve the way the reader thinks, feels, and behaves, ultimately assisting the reader in evolving into an emotionally resilient human being.

As Dr. Barry says, emotional resilience can be fostered by:

- Recognize that our thoughts have an effect on our actions
- Recognize stress and be willing to deal with it efficiently
- Being receptive to change and adaptable to new situations
- Accepting the reality that simply altering our response to stress, significant improvements can be made
- Embracing the self through the development of self-compassion and empathy.

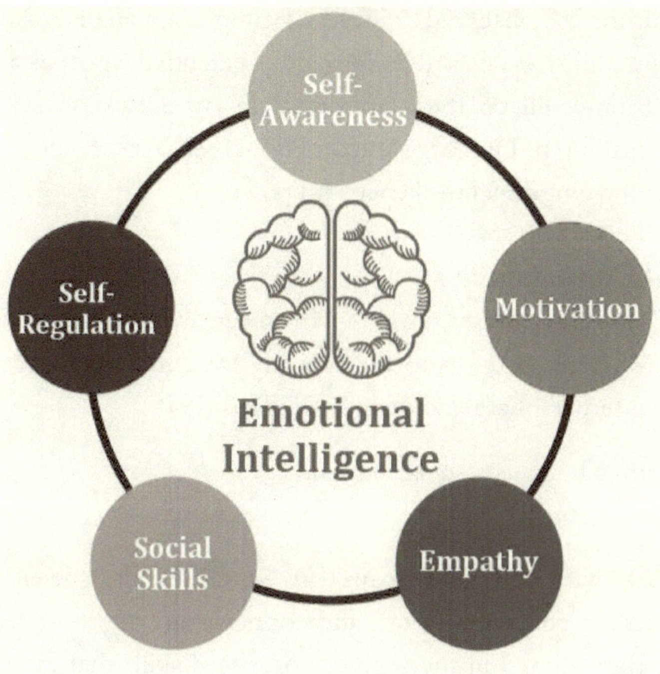


## The Major Findings of Dr. Harry Barry

Dr. Barry, who has over 35 years of experience as a therapist and psychologist, shared numerous reflections about depression, anxiety, and other psychological illnesses with us. However, most agree that this work on emotional resilience is his most significant contribution to the area of mental health to date.

Dr. Barry's book, 'Emotional Resilience: How To Protect Your Mental Health,' is divided into three sections. All of his findings are based on three skill sets he believes are critical for emotional resilience development. Among these skill sets are the following (Barry, 2018):

### *1. Personal Qualities*

The abilities necessary to manage our own lives — critical abilities such as self-acceptance, empathy, self-esteem, reasoning, problem-solving, anxiety and frustration management, procrastination management, and emotional regulation.

The author has observed countless examples of anxiety, sadness, low productivity, and stress disorders during his extended career as a therapist, and he attributes all of these abnormalities to a lack of certain basic talents. According to Dr. Barry, unconditional self-acceptance is necessary for developing emotional resilience and power.

## *2. Social Competence*

Social skills are described as the ability to engage well with oneself and with one's environment. It refers to the capacity for initiating and maintaining long-term interpersonal relationships (Phillips, 1978).

> "A human being is a social animal."
>
> \- Aristotle

We coexist with other humans in a close-knit society through communication, contact comfort, and cooperation.

Harry Barry noted in the segment on social skills that increasing our interactions with people, our perception of their difficulties, and our ability to adjust to them can help us build emotional resilience and prepare us to face burnouts positively.

His initiatives aimed at enhancing social skills include the following (Barry, 2018):

- Empathy development and practice in daily life - at work and at home
- Recognize and comprehend social cues – which are incorporated into both verbal and nonverbal communication
- Social anxiety and performance phobia management
- Utilizing the ability to express oneself

Life skills are the seamless integration of all of our social, personal, and cognitive abilities. It encompasses the ability to resolve a problem amicably, the capacity to handle and cope with stress effectively, and the capacity to achieve the ideal work-life balance. The training emphasizes the role of attention in emotional intelligence. Participants learn mindfulness practices and attention-focused techniques to cultivate the ability to stay present and attuned to their emotions and emotions of others. Quantum

Group highlights the connection between perception and emotional understanding. By exploring how individuals interpret and make sense of emotional cues, participants develop a heightened awareness of their own emotions and those of others, a fundamental aspect of emotional intelligence.

Dr. Barry has assured that by enhancing the collection of skills that belong under this area, one can undoubtedly become more emotionally resilient and well-adjusted. It is a relatively vast field that spans a large portion of our personality, and Barry has made it simple and relatable for readers to utilize in their daily lives with simple and realistic examples and activities.

The fact that we are in the midst of a 'anxiety endemic,' and that even children and adolescents are not immune, is the primary issue for which Dr. Barry developed the training methods and practical examples in the book.

## Dr. Barry's Suggestions

To enhance the aforementioned life skills that directly contribute to emotional resilience, he mentioned the following exercises (Barry, 2018):

1. Acceptance of oneself: Self-acceptance teaches us how to be more compassionate, courteous, and respectful of ourselves through practical examples.
2. Successfully overcoming procrastination: Dr. Barry identifies procrastination as a major impediment to emotional resiliency.

   This set of exercises is specifically developed for those who struggle with procrastination. It includes easy techniques such as letting go of the urge to be perfect, maintaining regular intervals when working long hours, and breaking down goals into smaller sub-goals.
3. Inundation: Anxiety, stress, and depression frequently present physically — with symptoms such as inexplicable headaches, insomnia, and palpitations.

   We can immediately confront our problems and strive to change them through 'Flooding,' a CBT strategy for confronting emotions.

Flooding has no boundaries or restrictions; each and every idea that we perceive as troubling is welcomed and addressed.

Only unconditional acceptance and a determination to resist them are required. This has been by far the most effective CBT strategy for developing resilience.

4. Striking a balance: Emotional resilience is a pattern of healthy functioning following a traumatic event. (2011) (Bonanno, Westphal, & Mancini).

It is the delicate balance that we can cultivate between our emotions and the extent to which we allow them to influence our lives. Dr. Barry noted in the part on life skills development that once we have gained the abilities necessary to cope with daily life challenges, we are already more emotionally robust.

To achieve the ideal balance in life, we can:

- Maintain a daily schedule in which we can record our daily duties and behave in accordance with the plan.
- Maintain a priority list and determine the relative importance of our children, partners, employment, parents, personal care, and social life.
- Return and re-establish our priorities as often as necessary.
- Commit to spending some quality time with those who are most important to you.
- Engage in active conversation with our partner on a regular basis to discuss the ups and downs of life and tackling issues rather than avoiding them.

## FIVE EXERCISES TO INCREASE EMOTIONAL RESILIENCE

> "The secret to mental and physical health is not to lament the past, fret about the future, or anticipate difficulties, but to live intelligently and earnestly in the current moment."
>
> \- Buddha

Developing emotional resilience entails the following:

- Constructing self-acceptance
- Enhancing stress management techniques
- Self-esteem development
- Being present-oriented and mindful
- Prudently expressing feelings

Choosing to respond to stress in a way that is not harmful to oneself or others

Here are a few exercises to assist you in addressing emotional resilience in daily life. Whether or whether you are currently battling and experiencing toxic stress, these simple daily actions can help you build your resilience.

1. Resilience Through the Positivity Effect

Allow yourself a few minutes to write down any five thoughts that are upsetting you at the moment. Make a note of them on a scrap of paper or in your device's notebook. Alongside the column where you've placed the negative thoughts, try substituting positive ones.For instance, "I am having difficulty managing my funds" can be substituted for "Let me seek financial help from friends and family." Simply by substituting written thoughts for verbal ones, you may observe how things might be seen differently.

The table below illustrates several instances of thinking replacement:

Alternative to Negative Thoughts Thoughts That Are Positive

1. This will never happen.
    1. I've saw worse times pass.
    2. My grip on life is slipping away from me.
    2. I am capable of regaining control.
    3. I am incapable of progressing.
    3. Perhaps I should allow some time.
    4. I will be unable to adapt in this location.
    4. Permit me to make some pals here.
    5. It is preferable to remain silent in order to avoid being judged.
    6. It's worth a shot

2. Gratitude Builds Resilience

   Gratitude is one of the most potent emotions that we can cultivate. When we learn to appreciate what we have rather than whine and fret about what we lack or what we have lost, we become more resilient.

Gratitude is centred on the concept of 'Stop, Look, and Go.' (Rast). Lack of gratitude immobilises us and saps our ability to recoil.

We can keep a thankfulness diary in which we record everything for which we are grateful, especially during stressful times. Filling in the columns of the journal will serve as a gentle reminder of all the positive aspects of life. A weekly journal might look like this:

We at Quantum Group recognize the integral connection between the normal functions of the brain, such as attention, perception, and other cognitive processes, and the development of Emotional Intelligence(EQ). Their programs can help participants understand the significance of these brain functions in enhancing EQ:

Quantum Group integrates insights from neuroscience into their programs, elucidating the relationship between brain functions and emotional intelligence. Understanding the neural underpinnings of attention, perception, and other cognitive processes provides a foundation for enhancing emotional awareness.

By understanding the interplay between normal brain functions and emotional intelligence, we at Quantum Group offer a comprehensive approach to EQ development. Participants gain insights into how attention, perception, memory and other cognitive processes shape emotional intelligence, ultimately empowering them to navigate their emotions and interpersonal relationships with greater skill and awareness.

* * *

Chapter 4

# From Self-control to Self-regulation: Building Emotional Resilience

| | **SELF**<br>Personal Competence | **OTHER**<br>Social Competence |
|---|---|---|
| **Recognition** | **Self-Awareness**<br><br>Emotional Self-Awareness<br>Accurate Self-Assessment<br>Self-Confidence | **Social Awareness**<br><br>Empathy<br>Service Orientation<br>Organizational Awareness |
| **Regulation** | **Self-Management**<br><br>Self-Control<br>Trustworthiness<br>Conscientiousness<br>Adaptability<br>Achievement Drive<br>Initiative | **Relationship Management**<br><br>Developing Others<br>Influence<br>Communication<br>Conflict Management<br>Leadership<br>Change Catalyst<br>Building Bonds<br>Teamwork and Collaboration |

Emotion processing is a non-conscious process. It is an intuitive process that enables us to anticipate others' behaviors more directly and immediately than language can. Immediacy is important to emotional intelligence. Our brains are wired in such a way that emotional responses can be processed without needing to evaluate them rationally. How am I feeling at the moment? How are you currently feeling? How are our emotions influencing one another and the behaviors we choose in this moment? These are the types of essential comparisons that the limbic system, or emotional brain, constantly makes for us, the majority of the time below the level of conscious awareness. When sensory information enters the brain, it is first processed in the thalamus, which searches it for recognizable patterns that may have been particularly meaningful to us in the past. These patterns are then passed to the hippocampus, which screens them further for potentially dangerous information before the amygdala makes the ultimate decision whether to initiate the fight-or-flight response. If there is no antecedent for dread, the information is then transferred to the neo cortex, which is capable of rationally analyzing it for significance. Additionally, the emotional circuits of the brain govern the balance of two essential chemicals in the body: cortisol and DHEA. Cortisol has numerous beneficial tasks in the body; yet, it is frequently referred to as the "stress hormone" because stressful conditions cause it to be generated in excess, which can have a negative influence on numerous areas of human health. DHEA, on the other hand, is sometimes referred to as the "anti-aging hormone" due to the way it counteracts cortisol's negative effects on the body, which tend to wear it down and cause it to age. The Coronary Heart Center says, the brain is not the only factor that influences our emotional intelligence. Indeed, recent research at the Institute of Heart Math (Children & Martin, 1999) shown that the heart plays a significant role in the process of comprehending and responding to our reality. Our heart communicates with the rest of our body chemically through the production of mood-enhancing hormones. Perhaps more astonishingly, the electromagnetic signal it transmits to the brain (and to every other cell) is the strongest signal in the entire body! It generates an electromagnetic field that may be detected in all directions several feet distant from the body. Additionally, the heart communicates mechanically with the rest of the body via pressure waves carried by the circulatory system. What is it transmitting through all of these disparate modes of communication? It provides feedback to the entire body on how the entire system is performing. According to Antonio Damasio's (2003) research, humans cannot make cognitive decisions without simultaneously processing emotional information about our feelings about the issue. Emotional intelligence, it turns out, is a combination of both heart and brain processes, weaving thought and emotion into the wondrously rich fabric of human experience.

## EMOTIONS AND SELF-IDENTIFICATION

Emotional intelligence is also crucial in resolving conflicts. Fisher and Ury (1981) characterize the process of resolving conflict as one of assisting people in moving from "No" to "Yes" in their What complicates matters is that we tend to identify with our positions, which means that changing them requires a shift in our identity. In other words, if we believe that we deserve the promotion and corner office as a result of our length and quality of service, we must alter our perception of who we are and what those rewards mean to us symbolically in order to embrace another (equally acceptable) alternative. This shift in identity may also occur as a result of going through a period of profound disappointment and finding how our capacities for flexibility and truth testing may actually assist us in transformation. Emotions are crucial for self-identification—for understanding who we are in the world and differentiating "self" from "other." Along with regulating the fight-or-flight response, the limbic system also regulates our immune system. The immune system's fundamental function is to discern between what is native to us and what is foreign. Even the process of discovering who we are is revealed to be biochemically based. Our cells have self-receptors that immune cells use to assess whether they are part of the self or invaders posing a threat to our systems' health, wholeness, and integrity. My own feeling of "I-ness" is derived on identifying familiar sensory patterns in the surroundings and experiencing the same emotional responses that were generated initially across my body/mind and stored in my memory. After a sufficient number of memories is stored (usually around the age of two), this sense of familiarity undergoes a major shift. The billions of pieces of data crystallize and commence the emergence of self, the understanding that this experience is being had by "I"—"I" who is hungry and wants to eat; "I" who feels safe, threatened, or curious; and "I" who is strong and can effect change in the world! Through this same process of associational memory, sophisticated menus of liking and aversion form over time. "I" learn that I am capable of expressing my preferences and dislikes successfully to the people on whom I rely for living. If I have grown up in a cooperative environment, family, or culture that demands me to get approval from others for all of my decisions and activities, my need for dependency will tend to outweigh my need for independence. If I've lived in a competitive atmosphere where I can only satisfy my goals by constantly developing and expressing new behavioral methods that violate the text of the law, my drive for independence will tend to outweigh my desire for interdependence. My ability to redesign, update, and even upgrade my identity, to settle problems and conflicts, and therefore to shift myself and others from "No" to "Yes," will be contingent upon how I process my emotions, whether consciously or unconsciously. If I am oblivious of the automatic sequence of stimulus-response conditioning, I am likely to be a creature of habit and to regard myself as a victim of the world. If I am able to increase the time between stimulus and response through self-reflective processes, in other words, if I am able to increase my awareness of the processes that determine my behavior, I will be more adaptable and tolerant, will have a more robust repertoire of behaviors available to me, and will be able to generate better decisions and more creative solutions to the problems I encounter in daily life. This is possibly the most accurate indicator of our emotional intelligence.

## ENHANCE YOUR EMOTIONAL STRENGTH

We need to debunk several popular fallacies regarding emotional intelligence and then establish the three strategic components necessary for relationship quality: tuning in, comprehending, and taking action.

Because our culture has conditioned us to interpret the world and value life in terms of objective attainment, we misunderstand and undervalue interpersonal connections. As a result, we require all assistance possible in developing, enhancing, and caring for our connectedness in ways that oppose this fragmentation. Fortunately, strategies for cultivating emotional intelligence have arrived just in time to begin re-weaving the frayed strands of postmodern society. Whether we seek such healing or not, the world will continue to get more complex, and the quality of our lives will be increasingly touched daily by the feelings and decisions of individuals we have never met or even seen. In a sense, each of us lives at the World Wide Web's center, and in order to keep all the connections in our network secure and beneficial, we must be extremely skilled in the way we generate and broadcast our emotional power—too much and people avoid us or build defenses that prevent communication; and they tend to take advantage of us, or we never break through the barriers to intimacy or develop enough energy to achieve the very dreams that give our lives meaning.

Emotional intelligence has long been recognized as a vital component of effective leadership. Our emotional intelligence competencies become increasingly critical as our leadership responsibilities increase. The primary goal in developing each of the four models is to establish an effective instrument for increasing awareness and so resulting in good change.

For example, a person who scores extremely well on reality tests but scores extremely low on optimism may choose to investigate how his or her view on life may alter if he or she did not instinctively spend so much attention to critical judgments. Could the individual be more optimistic? Consider what would happen if someone possesses a high level of assertiveness but a low level of impulse control. The Self-Perception composite measures self-esteem, self-actualization, and emotional self-awareness. These are the abilities necessary for effectively developing, maintaining, and comprehending oneself. Self-Expression is a composite term that encompasses Emotional Expression, Assertiveness, and Independence, all of which contribute to one's capacity to express oneself in a way that others will understand and promote engagement. The Interpersonal scale assesses our ability to interact and engage effectively within a social setting. Interpersonal Relationships, Empathy, and Social Responsibility comprise it. Problem Solving, Reality Testing, and Impulse Control are all components of the Decision Making composite. These assist us in integrating our emotional responses and awareness with our engagement and decision-making processes. The Stress Management scale assesses our perceptions of our ability to cope with the tension, disappointment, and discomfort inherent in living in a less-than-perfect world. The gap between what we seek and what we are capable of obtaining is what defines stress. Flexibility, Stress Tolerance, and Optimism are all components of stress management. Optimism demonstrates our optimism for the quality of the future we anticipate, while Flexibility and Stress Tolerance enable us to behave in accordance with our optimism. Happiness/Well-Being, which indicates how satisfied we feel in the present moment and is associated with the relevant abilities of Self-Regard, Optimism, Interpersonal Relationships, and Self-Actualization and self regard, all of which have a direct impact on our feeling of happiness.

## WHY SHOULD WE BE CONCERNED WITH SELFREGARD?

This is clearly analogous to the question, "Why should I care about myself?" Self-esteem is a vital competency because without a well-integrated identity that enables you to know and appreciate yourself, you will never be able to live truthfully, be truly reliable in work or love, or completely express all of your gifts. A lack of self-esteem frequently reflects emotions of insecurity and doubt, as well as a reluctance to enter into one's own environment and conduct.

## HOW CAN WE IMPROVE OUR SELF-CONTROL?

Take a position in front of the mirror. Consider the depths of your eyes. Three times with authority, call your name out loud, then remain silent and feel yourself show up! Now clap your hands madly and bow. How deserving or undeserving you feel of receiving good in your life is determined by a combination of factors, including your experiences, values, attitudes, behaviors, and expectations. You will perceive these conditions with varying degrees of accuracy, depending on your level of honesty and self-awareness. Whereas emotional self-awareness refers to how well you understand your feelings, self-esteem refers to how well you understand and appreciate the entire constellation of characteristics that make up who you are. This is largely decided by the consistency with which you convey your ideals and desires through your external actions. Because most of your reason to gravitate toward certain things and away from others is unconscious, developing a healthy self-esteem requires an ongoing process of self-discovery in order to continue discovering more of your total self and giving it more complete expression. It is impossible to hold oneself in the greatest respect if one is incapable of resolving personal problems or of asserting one's desires with sufficient force to satisfy them. Reciprocally, when one's self-esteem grows, one's problem-solving and assertiveness skills may also improve.

Given that self-esteem is one of the strongest indicators of competent conduct, the benefits of its development include a developing understanding of identity that is more rich, versatile, confident, and secure. As we continue to develop a more positive view of ourselves, we increase our potential to enjoy our lives and serve others.

Doris Lessing is a self-taught writer who was born in what is now Iran to British parents. She was born and reared in colonial Rhodesia, which is now Zimbabwe, and currently resides in London. She is an extraordinary writer and a 2007 Nobel laureate in literature, as well as the recipient of countless other honors. She is regarded an African writer, a women's writer, and has been dubbed "the archaeologist of human connections" by Irving Howe. In announcing the award in Stockholm in October 2007, the Swedish Academy described her as a "epicist of the female experience" who "has scrutinized a divided civilization with skepticism, fire, and imaginative strength." She is widely considered as one of the most significant post-1945 English-language writers. Her novels, short stories, and essays have addressed a variety of issues, ranging from the politics of race, which she confronted in her early novels set in Africa, to the politics of gender, which led to her adoption by the feminist movement, particularly for her novel The Golden Notebook, to the role of the family and individual in society, which she explored in her late 1970s and early 1980s space fiction. Lessing encourages us to examine ourselves as people and in relation to one another. Her unabashed eagerness to observe and report frequently cost her in a variety of ways, notably as a female writer at a time when such candor was frequently frowned upon. Nonetheless, her unflinching courage and determination to telling the truth as she saw it improved us as a people. Her positive self-esteem is critical to her ability to share her abilities.

## INCREASE SELF-AWARENESS

The definition of "Self-actualization" is the process of pursuing one's full potential in terms of capacity, abilities, and qualities. It necessitates the capacity and determination to set and attain goals. It is defined by involvement in and commitment to a variety of hobbies and pursuits. Self-actualization is a life-long endeavor that results in life enrichment" (2001, p. 89). Abraham Maslow, a psychologist, was perhaps the first to identify self-actualization as a skill. Maslow (1970), writing in the mid-twentieth century, developed a hierarchy of fundamental needs, each of which must be addressed adequately before proceeding to the next phase. The hierarchy progresses from physiological requirements (food, shelter, and water) to safety (security, order, and law) to belongingness and love needs (giving and receiving affection) to esteem needs (self- and other-esteem) and lastly to self-actualization. Maslow highlighted the importance of living up to one's potential in order to avoid dissatisfaction. Self-actualization is the process of being loyal to one's own nature and dedicating oneself entirely to the development of one's potential. It encompasses ideas such as development, motivation, and achieving our "being" requirements. Maslow later reinterpreted self-actualization as a function of peak experiences, which is why some people equate self-actualization with mystical experiences. While those fortunate enough to have mystical experiences are undoubtedly on the path to self-actualization, there are numerous more everyday manifestations of this ability. According to Maslow, self-actualization is most likely the next and ultimate phase after EI in the complicated process of personal growth, While emotional intelligence is associated with effectiveness, self-actualization is associated with doing your best. According to Bar-2001 On's article, "the best predictors of self-actualization are the following eight EI variables, given in ascending order of importance: Happiness Optimism Self-esteem Self-reliance Solving problems Social responsibility Assertiveness Self-awareness on an emotional level". What a powerful illustration of the critical nature of developing all aspects of our emotional intelligence! Self-actualization refers to our sense of accomplishment in pursuing the goals that make life meaningful for us personally. This capacity to derive meaning from the most difficult and even violent aspects of human experience demonstrates the human spirit's incredible resilience. We are focused on self-motivation in this work since it, when paired with strengths in happiness and optimism, as well as the other six abilities, enables us to live an energized and fully involved life. Self-actualization is a process, not a goal. It is the interface between our "doing" and "being" modes. Thus, the critical questions are as follows: How am I faring on this adventure? How am I conducting myself on this journey? Am I content with my current situation? Am I maintaining a steady pace during this journey? Am I driven to be the best version of myself?

## WHY SHOULD WE CONCERN OURSELVES WITH SELFACTUALIZATION?

We all have a deep inner want to be the best versions of ourselves. This may be a loud and urgent yell for some of us, or a faint whisper for others. Our current level of happiness, optimism, and the other six elements that contribute to self-actualization will influence our desire to develop this talent and our belief in its possibility. If we have a pessimistic disposition, we narrow our sense of potential and miss several opportunities. Perhaps even the pessimist can remark to himself or herself, "Well, IF it were possible..." This is the way to realizing our dreams, to finding meaning in our lives—one day at a time. For today's successful enterprises, self-actualization is crucial. Each year, millions of dollars are spent on team development and staff development to assist employees develops their motivation to be the best they can be. Self-actualization, in this very practical sense, is critical to organizational success.

## HOW CAN WE IMPROVE OUR SELF-CONCEPTUALIZATION?

Bear in mind that self-actualization is a process of progress. Motivate yourself to be the best version of yourself today. Do not be discouraged if you have not completed everything by today; instead, watch success unfold! Take note of your longings and the subtle messages you send to yourself. Are you a banker who aspires to be an artist—or vice versa? This EI ability is built upon eight other abilities; hence it is not a stand-alone capability. It is an integral aspect of one's identity. It is critical to identify which abilities are most beneficial to us and which might be enhanced to aid in our self-actualization. This is not a race; this is an evolutionary process. If you purposefully go forward on a regular basis, one step at a time, while maintaining the vision as a possibility, you will be able to listen to your inner knowledge and experience significantly greater progress than if you are constantly feeling guilty for not "doing more." After all, the "shoulds" have been phased out—they belong to the previous century. This is a period of opportunity.

## SELF AWARENESS OF ONE'S'EMOTIONS

Understanding your emotions and why you feel the way you do is possibly the most crucial component of emotionally effective living. It is inextricably linked to our capacity for empathy, or our ability to comprehend what other people are feeling and why they feel the way they do. Together, these two abilities—emotional awareness and empathy—allow us to inspire and influence our own and others' ideas and actions—in short, the talents necessary for success in life. Consider for a moment the reality that emotions are inextricably linked to sensation; indeed, our emotional lives begin when babies and infants explore their physical world. Until we are strong enough to turn over in bed, we are mostly at the mercy of our environment's conditions. When anything pokes or constrains us, we are unable to locate or change it. Nevertheless, our bodies show aversion reflexively by constricting their muscles—at first at the site of discomfort, then across the limb or trunk, and finally throughout the entire body if the sensation is severe enough. If none of this alleviates our discomfort, we cry out for assistance! When we are pleased with something, such as a warm bottle or someone rocking us in his or her arms, our muscles normally relax to allow us to enjoy the sensation. Obviously, feeding demands some muscular activity (which is also predominantly reflexive), but maybe more intriguing is the fact that enjoyment itself requires a type of "effort" called awareness. Consciously perceiving the feelings we are experiencing is analogous to pressing the "record" button on our life recorders and bringing the sensory experience's memories to consciousness. In comparison, feeding sensations may be recorded unconsciously due to their reflexive nature or consciously if the infant is aware and paying attention to the sensory experience.

## WHY ARE WE INTERESTED IN EMOTIONAL SELF-AWARENESS?

This brings us to the point. Emotions begin with the values we develop for our sensory experiences, our preferences and dislikes. Our ability to detect and express our emotional preferences is dependent on the circumstances surrounding our pleasant and unpleasant emotions. All of our sensory life is recorded in us, and the way we recall those emotions—whether more consciously and intentionally or more unconsciously and reactively—is entirely dependent on our level of emotional self-awareness. Following sensory and emotional awareness, the next stage of development is symbolic awareness, in which we begin to transform our experiences into the words and concepts of our native language. This is an extraordinarily fulfilling and exciting period of our lives! By this time, we've developed the muscular power and coordination enough to explore our world (more or less) at the whim of our own interest… and we're able to communicate our desires and needs much more precisely. Unfortunately, the ability to objectify our world through language and operate on it as "other than ourselves" is frequently over emphasized and reinforced as we begin to think about our children's future in terms of the goals they will need to achieve in our technologically driven postmodern society. As parents, we are busy, our attention is divided between a dozen different tasks, we are attempting to attain our own definitions of success, and we are exhausted. If we do not know how to model the emotional world's integration with the symbolic world intentionally, our children may wind up reacting out of their conditioned emotional preferences rather than responding with emotional intentionality, or emotional intelligence.

We at Quantum Group are committed to empowering individuals on their journey towards self-autonomy, meeting their needs up to self-actualization, and building a strong self-esteem. Here's how our programs can facilitate this transformative process:

Quantum Group conducts workshops that guide participants through self –discovery processes. These sessions help individuals understand their values, strengths, and areas for growth, laying the foundation for building self-autonomy. The training programs incorporate a needs-based approach inspired by Maslow's hierarchy of needs. Quantum Group helps participants identify and prioritize their needs, offering strategies to fulfill these needs and create a stable foundation for self-actualization.

## HOW CAN WE IMPROVE OUR EMOTIONAL AWARENESS?

To help our children and ourselves develop the ability to express emotional self-awareness deliberately, we need to connect with many aspects of our experience—what we're experiencing, why we're feeling that way. We can find and convey our interior experience with a very simple language pattern proposed by Robert Carkhuff in his 1970s human relations training: "I feel, because. "

1 "I'm concerned since I'm unable to contact my daughter."
2 "I'm enraged that you misled me."
3 "I'm ecstatic because I've never seen a roller coaster that large."

We must routinely check in with ourselves and measure our emotional pulse, and then, if necessary, share what we learn with those around us.

## Benefits

Without emotional self-awareness, we will react rather than initiate. It will appear to us as if we are at the mercy of life rather than capable of effectively influencing it on our own behalf and that of those we care about. Reconnecting with our sensory and emotional awareness and deliberately engaging it not only assists us in achieving our goals in life, but also enables us to appreciate them much more fully. It will help us to respond to the situation.

# EMOTIONAL EXPRESSION

Emotional awareness is a measure of our sensitivity to our emotional energy and our ability to detect our emotions, emotional expression is a measure of our ability to transmit our feelings appropriately and effectively to others. Apart from being as dissimilar to speaking as listening is to speaking, there is also a requirement for a well-diversified emotional lexicon that enables us to interpret our sensory data into verbal expression. To do this effectively, individuals must have a sufficient number of emotion terms at their disposal to appropriately discern the large diversity of emotional states that comprise team environment. This encompasses not only fundamental distinctions like as exhilaration vs discouragement, but also varying degrees of intensity within a single emotion. Are the employees content to be there or are they fervently committed to success? Are they apprehensive that the beta test may have to be extended or that the product may never operate as promised?

Cultivating Positive Self-Esteem: Quantum Group addresses the importance of cultivating a positive self-esteem. Through affirming exercises, feedback mechanisms, and positive psychology principles, participants learn to appreciate their worth and capabilities, contributing to a resilient and positive self-image.

## HOW SHOULD I BE CONCERNED WITH EMOTIONAL EXPRESSIVENESS?

Emotions communicate values. Our bodies will not generate an emotional response unless there is something valuable in the world that we should be aware of. It could be a negative value that we must avoid at all costs or a positive value that we must seize. It could be that something is impeding us from achieving a goal to which we are completely devoted, signaling that we need to step up our efforts to overcome the impediment. It could be a chance to offer, to assist another individual or group in overcoming big obstacles they face but are unable to overcome on their own.

## HOW CAN WE IMPROVE OUR EMOTIONAL EXPRESSIVITY?

Certainly, expanding our emotional language is a critical step toward boosting our emotional expressiveness. If we lack the vocabulary to express the subtleties of our emotions, it will be difficult for others to consciously comprehend what we are feeling. It is vital, however, to remember that our nonverbal communication is always communicating to them whether we are happy or angry, whether we feel threatened or are threatening. Increased emotional expressiveness demands the self-confidence that comes with self-esteem and the boldness that comes with assertiveness; therefore, increasing those two abilities may be important if we are to express our feelings more openly and truthfully. Effective emotion expression also requires us to be more deliberate with our nonverbal expressions. Our posture, tone of voice, facial expression, gestures, volume and rhythm of our speech, and other nonverbal cues communicate more than 90% of the signals we send. Only roughly 7% of the whole is composed of words. Due to the fact that the majority of our nonverbal communication is unconscious, we may unknowingly transmit our own fear, anger, or judgment in ways that diminish our influence rather than more successfully elicit the attention and cooperation of others around us.

## CONCERN FOR EXPRESSION

When something is important to you, encourage yourself to express it respectfully rather than burying your emotions. Suggestion: They should take note of how they are feeling and why, and tell themselves discreetly. Take a deep breath and regain your composure. "I feel because," you can say to others. For a stretch objective, they can then reciprocate and investigate how and why others are experiencing.

Humans have four primary motivations: want, fear, anger, and compassion. They are the catalysts for our actions. We go toward what we seek in order to achieve it; we move away from what we fear or detest; and we move against the objects, policies, and people that stand in our way. When we are motivated by altruistic sentiments, we gravitate toward people and events that matter to us in order to share the emotional and physical resources we possess. Understanding the relationship between emotions and motivation enables us to read others more correctly and communicate more deliberate and readily received messages.

## SELF ASSERTIVENESS

Assertiveness is the capacity to communicate one's opinions, beliefs, and thoughts in a nondestructive manner and to protect one's rights. Assertiveness is composed of three fundamental components:

1. The capacity to express feelings (for example, the capacity to accept and express anger, warmth, and sexual feelings);
2. The capacity to express beliefs and thoughts openly (the capacity to express opinions, disagree, and take a definite stand, even when doing so is emotionally difficult or when there is something at stake); and
3. The capacity to advocate for personal rights (not allowing others to bother you or take advantage of you). Assertive individuals are not too self-conscious or bashful; they are capable of expressing their feelings (often immediately) without being confrontational or abusive." Weisinger (1998, p. 122) defines assertiveness as "the capacity to stand up for your rights, opinions, ideas, beliefs, and needs while still respecting those of others." The concept of negative space can aid in our comprehension of the distinction between assertiveness

and aggression. Artists and designers employ the concept of negative space to convey information about an object's shape, contour, and contextual meaning. This is performed by examining the space in which the thing resides. For instance, if you're drawing a pear, move your gaze slightly away from it to observe how the pear blocks and shadows the space or objects surrounding it. This is an effective technique for evaluating a concept. To investigate a concept's negative space, consider what it is not. This assists in minimizing erroneous assumptions and erroneous conclusions. Assertiveness is not synonymous with aggression. Aggression progresses beyond assertiveness to include obtrusiveness, combativeness, and militancy. The critical distinction between the two is that aggression makes no allowance for consideration of others' feelings, perspectives, or intentions. Aggressiveness is defined by a will to win at all costs. The image of steamrolling over someone perfectly captures aggression. Assertiveness is an expressive behavior that respects the dignity and humanity of others, even when expressing an undesired or contentious message. The bottom line is that assertiveness occupies the middle ground between being a pushover and being a steamroller.

## WHY SHOULD I BE CONCERNED WITH ASSERTIVENESS?

Assertiveness is our backbone, spine, spunk, or chutzpah—our capacity to interact with and make our voices heard in our environment! Assertiveness strengthens us and aids in our self-definition. It contributes to our sense of self-esteem because we are expressing our desires, feelings, and thoughts and clearly defining our boundaries. While assertiveness begins on the inside by addressing our own emotions and responses, it eventually shows in our communication and behavior. We are frequently forced to be aggressive and to voice dangerous positions in order to communicate effectively. According to the authors of Skilled Interpersonal Communication, assertive communication is "standing up for oneself while also considering the other person." The assertive approach entails… expressing personal feelings and opinions honestly and firmly; valuing oneself on an equal footing with others; and being willing to listen to the other's point of view. Individuals are constantly confronted with divergent views and conflicts. To be effective in our own lives, whether at work or at home, we must address difficulties and resolve disagreements in an appropriate manner. Lynn Eisaguirre states in The Power of a Good Fight, "We need to move toward embracing conflict as a friendly force to be controlled and used, rather than avoided like the enemy." Leadership entails developing an appreciation for confrontation". How much happier and more effective would we be if we could consistently articulate our positions while maintaining, or even deepening, relationships in high-risk situations? Assertiveness enables us to be authentic and respectful of others.

## HOW CAN WE INCREASE OUR ASSERTIVENESS?

Typically, developing assertiveness entails the following: Constructing it—from reluctance reducing it—from aggression to begin, ascertain your position on a continuum. When assertiveness is required, do you remain silent or do you kick into high gear? When you are not forceful enough, do you constantly gravitate toward one end of the continuum or bounce back and forth depending on the situation? They assist us in regulating our behavior at both extremes of the spectrum. Empathy enables us to be more receptive to the perspectives of others and mitigates our defensiveness. It makes it simpler to treat others with decency and respect. Additionally, it will assist us in considering how the knowledge we are withholding from them may benefit their growth. Courage enables us to take on further dangers. It has the ability to rekindle our spirit when we are feeling timid. It can also assist us in being more receptive to alternative viewpoints.

## NOT PASSIVE, BUT ASSERTIVE

How does assertiveness feel? Are you more effective when your assertiveness is activated? Improved assertiveness skills have the potential to tremendously raise our worth, impact, and well-being. When we use them gracefully, we are neither victims nor weapons of mass destruction. We do not make ourselves ill by holding ill will against others and repressing unpleasant emotions. Nor do we inflict illness on others by erupting all over them in an obnoxious and caustic manner. The graceful application of assertiveness empowers us to be empowered individuals who confront issues head-on and can be relied upon for clarity and candor. Organizations are more productive when managers and employees use appropriate assertiveness and communicate openly about issues and facts.

## AUTONOMY

Independence is the capacity to think independently of another' thoughts, desires, and feelings. This does not imply utter insensitivity to the needs of others or to societal mores. This implies that an individual is capable of sorting through the input and expectations of others, accessing his or her own views and values, and then arriving at conclusions and doing actions that make sense for his or her own life. The degree of independence deemed suitable and the manner in which it is manifested are culturally determined. Eastern societies place a premium on communal processes over individual needs, whereas Western cultures place a premium on individualism. The cowboy, an enduring American icon, is the ideal embodiment of independence. It can be challenging to think and act independently. The phrase "groupthink" refers to the act of adhering to another's values and ethics. Groupthink, as the polar opposite of independence, precludes uniqueness. Independent is defined by Webster's Dictionary as "(1) not subject to external control: not subordinate; not associated with or integrated into a larger governing organization"

## WHY SHOULD WE BE CONCERNED WITH INDEPENDENCE?

The capacity to stand on one's own two feet and trust one's own judgment is defined as independence. It demonstrates self-assurance and a readiness to take chances. Independence is a critical leadership characteristic that can boost performance regardless of whether one is the CEO of a multinational corporation, the supervisor of a small team, a parent, a volunteer with a community group, or the leader of one's own life. Independence is necessary in a team context, as long as it is conveyed sensitively and with a collaborative attitude. When an individual is able to take initiative and accomplish tasks while involving others and contributing to the group's collective efforts, he or she is appreciated as a team member.

## HOW CAN WE IMPROVE OUR INDEPENDENCE?

Take note of the times and places in your life where you are hesitant to assert your independence. Is it true in all scenarios or only in specific situations with specific people? Investigate what makes you feel uneasy about exerting your independence. Are you concerned that others will perceive you as "unique"? Will others become enraged? Is there a possibility that your viewpoint or conclusion will be contested? Ask others the same questions (s). Determine the risk associated with acting autonomously. If there is more to gain (self-esteem, confidence, and enhanced teamwork) from asserting independence, then establish a step-by-step plan to facilitate its development. If you follow through on the plan, you will discover that you are confronting your anxieties about independence and building your capacities.

## THE PLEASURES OF INDEPENDENCE

Consider your first two-wheeled bicycle: It originally came equipped with training wheels, but those were removed. You were reduced to two wheels and your father gripping the back of your seat as you pedaled. Finally, you experienced the liberation of completing the task entirely on your own. What an adrenaline thrill!!

A person who effectively utilizes independence will have the satisfaction of knowing that he or she behaves in accordance with his or her sense of ethics and values and avoids unhealthy pressure to comply. These individuals are not only puppets on a string. Each time an individual adheres to his or her convictions and intuition, the independence response is strengthened. When difficult problems emerge, he or she will have the fortitude to overcome them.

Mahatma Gandhi was a British barrister who campaigned for civil liberties and independence in South Africa and India. He operated according to his own moral compass and defied cultural standards. His lifetime struggle was against religious, caste, and racial biases. He abstained from violence and achieved fame in the social arena by individual resistance and non-cooperation. "Gandhi possessed an uncommon aptitude for resisting wrong and for loving his adversaries, which perplexed his adversaries and compelled their admiration" (www.MKGandhi.com, 2003). He was the catalyst for India's independence from British domination.

## INTERPERSONAL RELATIONSHIPS

Interpersonal relationships are where emotional intelligence is put to the test; they are where the rubber meets the road. Our ability to form interpersonal interactions determines whether the people in our lives look forward to seeing us or fear it. Here, our needs, aspirations, and expectations are anticipated, acknowledged, valued, and treated with respect, or they are hindered and neglected. Our interpersonal ties shape the social and emotional climates of our families, neighborhoods, and workplaces. When our connections are healthy, they give the common ground on which we can share our own experience of humanness. Some have described interpersonal competence as "the capacity to develop and maintain mutually satisfying relationships that are defined by the capacity to 'give' and 'take' in partnerships and by an open expression of trust and compassion in words or conduct." The confounding aspect is the demand for mutuality. To develop truly mutually rewarding relationships, we must relinquish some of our authority to another individual or group of people. However, as a result of the inherent relationship between emotional competences, we realize that this type of surrender is also required for social responsibility! Nothing will focus our interest and attention more than giving up part of our own self-interest and having, as they say, "some skin in the game." To establish a really mutual connection, we must understand the other person well enough to anticipate their preferences and be able to satisfy them to some level... and they become the last arbiter of our success or failure! To complicate matters further, there are moments when nearly everyone is slightly deceitful about what they want and what they are or are not ready to provide. For a relationship to have actual depth, we must eventually get to know the other person well enough to understand when he or she is bluffing and to constructively extract the other person's honest opinion when it matters and when it doesn't.

## WHY ARE INTERPERSONAL RELATIONSHIPS IMPORTANT?

Regardless of our denials, humans must care about interpersonal relationships because we are primates, who are by nature very social creatures. We cannot survive in isolation for an extended period of time. Our ancestors' biology predisposes us to seek social interaction. All of the structures in your brain and heart, as well as the neurotransmitters that circulate throughout your body, are derivatives of millions of years of activity. You cannot avoid the desire to be touched, held, and spoken to. Unless you suffer from one of the more severe forms of mental dysfunction such as schizophrenia or autism, you cannot avoid seeking reflections of yourself in other human beings. As the globe gets more crowded and more of our resources must be shared, our capacity to make and maintain friends is vital to our social advancement—and maybe survival. Mutual trust and commitment among neighbors and community members were critical components of the American Revolution's success and the settlement of the frontier. It is only as our wealth has increased that we have been able to afford the level of separation and fragmentation that has become typical. There are significant expenses associated with this estrangement. We have a vague sensation of competition with our neighbors, even distrust, and a wish to avoid their intrusions. What may surprise those of us who have been conditioned to believe that success comes from competition and winning is that reinvesting more of our resources and concern in social responsibility not only costs us nothing, but actually increases our stress tolerance and makes us happy. By taking a more objective, honest look at ourselves, we learn that we are social beings by nature.

## HOW ARE INTERPERSONAL RELATIONSHIPS BUILT?

"Friendship should be more than the severance that Time can bring." Murder in the Cathedral, T.S. Eliot Fortunately, the skills necessary for developing long-lasting, mutually beneficial relationships are well-known and easily practiced by individuals who genuinely choose to grow. Additionally, this is the skill that is most susceptible to hereditary limits imposed by a biological set point, out of the sixteen. Each of us has a general zone of comfort that dictates our level of reserve or outgoingness. We can learn to operate independently of that, but we will need to replenish our batteries. The first step is to honestly assess your existing level of contentment. Consider the important relationships in your life and consider the greatest and least satisfying parts. The second stage is to acknowledge that if you want to create new friends or improve the quality of an existing relationship, you must change. Attempting to change or improve the other person is never a worthwhile goal; rather, it is a surefire prescription for frustration and failure. The third step is to begin practicing specific activities, such as developing your listening skills, introducing yourself to others, identifying areas of mutual interest, understanding nonverbal clues, and concluding discussions in a way that encourages future contact. Certain relationships, on the other hand, should be abandoned rather than improved—abusive partnerships fall into this group. Knowing which connections to cultivate and which to let go is a distinct talent, and there are numerous resources available on the subject. Here, we'll discuss how to initiate and strengthen healthy relationships.

Improving your interpersonal relationship skills can result in a variety of benefits, ranging from stress reduction to enhanced productivity and creativity, as well as an increased sense of happiness in life. Celebrating your accomplishments is a critical component of happiness development.

Increase the amount and quality of your interpersonal ties, and you'll have more people with whom to celebrate your accomplishments! As you support your customers in developing this ability, they are likely to see an increase in their ease and success in accomplishing their desired goals.

## CONCLUSION

Thus emotional intelligence starts as soon as we come to this world and grows with us as we grow. It is an inevitable part of us which needs training and development. We must know our reality and be able to live in the now, the present situation. It includes our physical, psychological and spiritual behavior.

It is learning to live one day at a time and one thing at a time. If you try to embrace all your problems at one time you will not succeed. Similarly if go at little by little you will go through easily. Keeping things simple, being conscious of our own self, our thoughts, feelings, reasoning and our responses or for that matter reactions.

Having only a high IQ is not enough to be successful in life. A high EQ is equally important. It is a known fact that if a person has a high EQ he can live a good life even if he is not educated.

> *'Not to self: This is your journey, your body, your mind, and your spirit. Dig deep, own it and start doing things for you and by you."*

* * *

www.ingramcontent.com/pod-product-compliance
Lightning Source LLC
LaVergne TN
LVHW091118150826
845673LV00002B/886

* 9 7 9 8 8 9 2 3 3 5 2 0 1 *